THE ELEMENT GUIDE

DEPRESSION

Sue Breton is an experienced clinical psychologist and author working in a busy private practice in Wales. She has spent many years helping people with many difference sorts of depression. She is also the author of *Why Worry* (Element).

THE ELEMENT GUIDE SERIES

The Element Guide series provides clear, practical advice on psychological and emotional states to bring help and guidance to sufferers and their families.

In the same series

Anorexia & Bulimia by Julia Buckroyd
Anxiety, Phobias & Panic Attacks by Elaine Sheehan
Bereavement by Ursula Markham

• THE ELEMENT GUIDE •

DEPRESSION

Your Questions Answered

Sue Breton

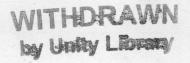
ELEMENT

Shaftesbury, Dorset • Rockport, Massachusetts
Brisbane, Queensland

First published in Great Britain in 1996 by
Element Books Limited
Shaftesbury, Dorset SP7 8BP

Published in the USA in 1996 by
Element Books, Inc.
PO Box 830, Rockport, MA 01966

Published in Australia in 1996 by
Element Books Limited
for Jacaranda Wiley Limited
33 Park Road, Milton, Brisbane 4064

Reprinted 1997

7/98

Cover design by Max Fairbrother
Page design by Roger Lightfoot
Typeset by Footnote Graphics, Warminster, Wiltshire
Printed and bound in Great Britain by
Biddles Limited, Guildford & King's Lynn

British Library Cataloguing in Publication
data available

Library of Congress Cataloging in Publication
data available

ISBN 1–85230–775–7

Note from the Publisher
Any information given in any book in *The Element Guide* series is not
intended to be taken as a replacement for medical advice. Any
person with a condition requiring medical attention should
consult a qualified medical practitioner or suitable therapist.

Contents

Introduction

Who has not, at some time or other, said, 'I am depressed'?

It is a line that slips off the tongue all too readily when we are bored or unhappy. But most of us, when we say that, do not mean we are clinically depressed, possibly wanting or needing treatment. A fairy godmother or genie of the lamp might be nice, so that we could be granted our wish to win the pools or whatever. But a trip to the psychiatrist – no way!

And yet, the very fact that you are reading this book suggests that either you or someone you care about has a problem with depression.

It is the aim of this book first to help you decide whether the particular form of depression with which you are involved is one which you might attempt to alleviate by yourself, or whether it is one that really will not improve very much or very rapidly without professional help. Secondly, it offers some guidance both for those who are depressed and for those who share their lives. In it, I have briefly described the different diagnostic categories of depression and outlined the usual symptoms associated with each.

This book is not necessarily an alternative to professional help. As I have already said, there are some kinds of depression for which psychiatric treatment is necessary, and it will be made very clear which these are. There are others which would be helped by a course of an appropriate anti-depressant from a GP, and some for which some therapy is desirable, and for which the approach outlined in this book may be helpful. Finally, there are some types of depression which will probably cure themselves, given time. The cure may be hastened, however, by following some of the advice contained here.

CHAPTER 1

Different Kinds of Depression

The way in which depressive illness is classified has been changed recently. In practice this is really only of interest to statisticians and researchers, but you may know of someone, a friend or relative perhaps, who was given a particular diagnosis under the old system and wonder how that relates to a diagnosis that someone receives now.

Until very recently, depression was classified as either reactive or endogenous. Reactive depression was believed to have been caused by a particular event in a person's life. In other words, the sufferer became depressed as a reaction to things that had happened, such as redundancy, bereavement, serious illness, etc.

Endogenous depression was the kind that came over one for no obvious reason, when, as far as one could recall, nothing had happened to make one depressed. Endogenous means 'coming from within' and such depressions were thought to be due to biochemical changes within the body, although nobody was sure what triggered them.

There were also people who had phases of being manic or euphoric, after which they sank into a phase of deep depression. This was called manic depressive psychosis.

These definitions are still useful. Depression is a form of what is known as a mood, or affective, disorder, because it is primarily concerned with a change in mood. There are many practitioners who still prefer the old system, and it makes no difference to treatment, but figure 1 attempts to show how the two systems compare.

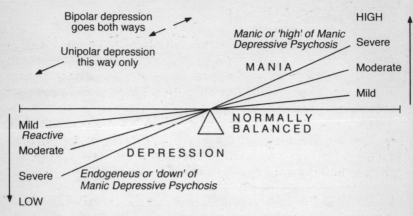

Figure 1 The Mood See-Saw

The main distinction that is made now is between unipolar and bipolar depressions. These definitions are not as complicated as they might seem at first. Unipolar simply means 'one-ended', and the term is used to describe all forms of depressive illness where the sufferer feels 'down'. Unipolar depressions do not have a manic phase. Depressed people who have such a phase are diagnosed as having a bipolar, or two-ended, depression.

This shift in classification has come about partly because research has shown that bipolar depressions, which feature both high and low phases – however mild or severe – have more in common with each other than they do with any of the disorders which feature only a depressed mood – the unipolar disorders.

Having decided whether the illness has only low phases or both highs and lows, the other classification deals with how severe these mood swings are (*see* figure 1).

Let us now consider the diagnoses one by one and see what the essential features of each are.

MOOD DISORDER

The first decision to be made is whether the person suffers *abnormal* moods, either manic or depressed. If so then he or she probably has some form of depressive illness. Even those who begin with unnaturally high moods will lapse into depression at some point.

Mild cases of either mania or depression alone may go unnoticed. People will often put them down to normal changes. In order to identify them as an illness it is necessary to look for other symptoms as well.

BIPOLAR AFFECTIVE DISORDER

This is the form of depressive illness in which the sufferer has periods of being on a high, as well as periods of depression. How severe these periods are may vary from person to person.

The term 'mania' is used to describe the severe forms of the high mood. In this condition the person shows psychotic symptoms, and may have hallucinations or delusions. Hallucinations are sensory experiences which do not really exist. The commonest form of hallucination is when people think they hear voices. These days sufferers often report that they are receiving messages especially for them via their television sets. Others become deluded into believing that they are someone important, such as the Queen or Napoleon. They will then act out their lives as if they were that person and will not realize that it is unreal. Their inability to see that what they are doing is illogical and irrational is called lack of insight.

This phase will usually come on suddenly and will last anything from two weeks to five months on average. When it goes, the person is once again as normal as ever.

The less severe form of high in bipolar disorder is hypomania. People with this form have increased energy and tend to become more active than usual. They do not, however, have delusions or hallucinations. They do not lose touch with reality in the sense that they know who they are and what is real. What can be a problem, however, is that they tend to overestimate their capabilities and fail to see the obvious risks involved in their ventures. For example, if they are in business, they may suddenly decide to expand in a way that is not really practical, or set up schemes for which they are ill prepared. Other forms of less inhibited behaviour include reckless driving, spending sprees, gambling and sexual adventures. They may also have lots of new ideas, but do not follow them through. They are often very jolly to be with but can become grumpy or impatient if they cannot do what they want.

I remember the case of Reginald, a country accountant. During a moderate manic phase he thought he would make more money for his practice and 'invested' a client's deposit with a bookmaker. The horse he backed won, so he decided to invest further.

Reginald's wife became concerned about his behaviour at home. He seemed restless and unable to concentrate on the TV or newspaper in the evenings, as he usually did. He also seemed to have wakeful nights and woke up earlier and earlier, then prowled around the house doing nothing in particular. His wife assumed that he was worried about work, but when she suggested as much to his partner at a social event, the partner insisted that Reginald appeared fine.

In fact it turned out that Reginald and his partner saw little of one another during their working hours, but that when they did, Reginald seemed cheerful. This was an outward manifestation of his mania, but it passed unrecognized because none of those closest to him, neither his wife nor his partner, could see the whole picture.

Eventually things got out of hand and Reginald began to lose more than he was winning. Finally, in desperation, he flew to the south of France one weekend and tried to win back everything he had lost in the casinos of Monte Carlo.

It is not unusual, however, for someone in a manic

phase also to experience symptoms which are more often associated with the depressive phase. Such symptoms may be agitation, an inability to concentrate on anything, and disinterest in some aspects of life, particularly sex.

The same thing may occur during the depressive phase of bipolar disorder: sufferers may show some manic symptoms, particularly overactivity and excessive talking.

The depressive phase of bipolar affective disorder may last up to six months. The symptoms are similar to those of the unipolar depressions described on pages 6 and 7. Any depressive disorder in which there is a manic phase, however slight, is likely to be a recurrent one; it is not usual to find people who have only a single such episode in their lives.

UNIPOLAR AFFECTIVE DISORDER

Unipolar disorder consists of periods of depression of varying degrees of severity. Whether the episode is classified as mild, moderate or severe depends both on the number of different symptoms present and also on the type of symptoms and their severity. For instance, a depression which features hallucinations and delusions would almost certainly be regarded as severe.

Another guide to severity is the degree to which the sufferer can carry on with their normal life. The less they are able to do so, the more severe the illness.

In order for a disorder to be classified as depression, there has to be evidence of lowered mood. This lowered mood may vary slightly throughout the day but the sufferer cannot usually be cheered up, and this is the major distinction between simply being unhappy and being clinically depressed. Merely unhappy people can be dragged out of their mood by circumstances, by friends or by something good that happens. Depressed people are largely unaffected by happy events. Their mood does not lift in response to what goes on around them. They generally remain what is termed emotionally flat and unresponsive.

Depressive episodes, however severe, feature some or all of the following symptoms:

- Loss of interest in, or the inability to take pleasure from, activities that are normally enjoyed, or found enjoyable by others. There is also a lack of desire to be involved in things which previously gave pleasure. Loss of interest in sex is also a feature of depression.
- Reduced ability to concentrate, which also causes impaired memory for everyday things, such as forgetting what they went upstairs to fetch. This is not so much due to a defect of memory, but because their lack of concentration has prevented their brains from registering what they were supposed to remember in the first place. Sufferers may find that they take longer than usual to absorb information or to work things out. Fairly simple tasks like making a cake, programming the video recorder, going round the supermarket or cleaning the car can require a real effort and may even be abandoned as being too taxing.
- Disturbed sleep. Many depressed people lack energy and become easily tired, yet do not sleep well at night. It is common to want to go to bed early but then to wake during the early hours and be unable to get back to sleep even though they feel tired. Many depressed people feel more depressed first thing in the morning and do not want to get up.
- Appetite variations. Most people lose interest in food as well as in everything else when depressed. There are some, however, who have a craving to 'comfort eat', and indulge themselves with carbohydrates such as chocolates, cakes and chips. Weight varies depending on the desire for food.
- Reduced self-esteem and self-confidence. It is thought by some workers in the field that low self-esteem may be a feature of people who are susceptible to depression,

even if they are not actually depressed. They argue that it simply becomes more pronounced during a depressive episode. Low self-esteem is discussed further in Chapter 3.

- Ideas of guilt and unworthiness. These too could be related to the sufferer's low self-esteem. In severe depressive episodes these feelings of unworthiness may be accentuated by hallucinations in the form of voices which tell the sufferer how worthless they are.

- Bleak and pessimistic views of the future. This symptom occurs with varying degrees of severity. The depressed person tends to distort future possibilities so as to project the worst possible scenario. This is one of the major difficulties to overcome in the treatment of depression. As is mentioned further in Chapter 4, pessimistic thoughts in themselves can keep you depressed.

- Ideas or acts of self-harm or suicide. This symptom is linked to the previous ones. Because the sufferer feels unworthy, and sees the future in bleak terms, he or she feels there is little point in going on living. They think about suicide and ways of committing it, even though they may not actually do anything about it.

- Loss of feelings. This refers to the sufferer's loss of any desire to express affection for, or interest in, others. Their only emotion seems to be a flatness which is best described by imagining a very bad amateur actor, who tries to play a role by just saying the words and performing the actions, without any feeling behind them.

- Reduced tolerance. Some sufferers find that they are less able to put up with noise and bright lights than usual.

The symptoms shown, and their severity, will depend on the degree of depression.

Mild Depression

This may feature any of the symptoms described above, and will, of course, always be characterized by a depressed mood. The sufferer will also show a diminished interest in things which he or she usually finds interesting or enjoyable.

Because this is only the mild form of the disorder, the symptoms are not very severe. Sufferers may carry on with their normal lives, only appearing low in spirits and possibly less sharp in their thinking or in their interest. They may stop doing things they do not actually have to do, but will often continue with the essentials, such as going to work or caring for the family. However, they will tend not to be as conscientious about these things as previously, or will become upset because they feel they are not coping as well as they should because they feel too tired.

Moderate Depression

More of the symptoms are present than are found in the mild form and they are usually more obvious. Sufferers may find it very difficult to continue with their job or with everyday chores and may well abandon them.

Severe Depression

In this condition sufferers will probably not function with any degree of reliability. They will tend to lack any desire to talk to others or to look after themselves. They may show a great deal of restlessness and general agitation, but will not do anything constructive. All their movements will be pointless.

In some cases the feelings of unworthiness and self-disgust may lead sufferers to 'hear voices'. These tell them that they are no good in some way, or that they have done terrible things. They may also believe that they have had visitations from the devil or other dark forces. People in this state are unable to lead any kind of normal life.

One major complication with depressive disorders is that, the more severe their symptoms, the less able sufferers are to motivate themselves to do anything about the problem. On the other hand, those with only the mild form of the disorder are inclined to feel that they are making a fuss about nothing and that they should try and 'pull themselves together'. They therefore do not always seek the help they need either.

Depression has a vicious downward spiral that sucks one in if one is not careful. The more depressed one feels, the less inclined one is to do anything positive and the deeper one sinks.

This is why the help of others is almost essential – but it has to be the right sort of help or it can make matters worse. I have tried to explain the help that is of most benefit to sufferers in Chapters 8 and 9.

CHAPTER 2

Other Disorders Featuring Depression

Apart from illnesses where depression is the main symptom, as described in Chapter 1, there are several other disorders where it also plays a part. These are included here because the advice can still be useful in coping with the depressive element.

RECURRENT BRIEF DEPRESSION

This is very similar to the examples of unipolar depression given in Chapter 1, except that it lasts a very short time. This leads those in the field to wonder whether it is a true depressive disorder or something completely different.

The average length of depressed mood in this disorder is only three days, and few episodes last for more than a week. Because they are so short, it has often been difficult to study them in any detail. It has been particularly difficult to assess the effects of anti-depressant drugs, since it takes two or three weeks for their effects to be seen, by which time a case of brief depression has got better.

One important aspect of this disorder, however, is that it is recurrent – it comes back. This means that the person will have another episode between one and five weeks later. In the course of a year episodes will recur about 12 to 20 times.

Although this disorder recurs about once a month, it is

not associated with a woman's menstrual cycle. Equal numbers of men and women seem to get it. The symptoms are much the same as those of other unipolar depressions.

As might be expected when one suffers such a disruptive and unpleasant disorder as frequently as this, the risk of suicide is very high.

The discovery of this disorder is recent and work is still in progress to discover more about it.

MASKED DEPRESSION

If you look back to the symptoms described on pages 6 and 7, you will see that some of them are psychological – for example loss of self-esteem, inability to concentrate and lack of feelings. Others are physical like disturbed sleep, changed appetite, loss of sex drive, slowed speech, slowed movements and thoughts, and intolerance of light and noise. It has been suggested that there may be a form of depression which goes unnoticed because, although the physical symptoms may be very similar, the psychological symptoms are lacking, or the person has not mentioned them for one reason or another. It is suggested that such disorders are due to the same or similar bodily causes as the other unipolar depressive illnesses (even though we do not yet know exactly what these causes are).

In the 19th century there was a disorder called neurasthenia, which was described as a disease in which the patient experienced severe fatigue. It was believed to be more common among the educated than the unskilled, and the cause was thought to be environmental – it was brought on by what are today regarded as stress factors such as emotional upset, bad experiences and overwork. The cure was said to be rest.

Neurasthenia is still diagnosed in Oriental countries such as Hong Kong, China and Taiwan. In the West, however, fatigue is seen to be a symptom of some other disorder rather than a disease in its own right.

It has been noted by some psychiatrists that what is currently known as chronic fatigue syndrome (CFS) bears a strong resemblance to what the Victorians called neurasthenia. CFS used to be termed 'yuppie flu' because it was first identified as a problem experienced by those who were striving to climb the ladder of success and it often occurred after the person had had a viral infection, such as flu. It was also known as ME, but chronic fatigue syndrome is now regarded as a better name on account of the symptoms.

Looking back, it is usually possible to identify some stress or pressure in the sufferer's life before the onset of this disorder. He or she also shows many of the physical symptoms of depression, but not often any of the psychological ones. This has led some mental health workers to suggest that it may indeed be a form of masked depression.

CFS sufferers are reluctant, however, to accept a psychiatric diagnosis because of the stigma which seems to be attached to this. There is still a belief amongst the general public that a physical disease is 'real' whereas a psychiatric one is in some way 'imaginary' or less respectable. I hope that this book, in which I will show the possible relationship between the mind and body in *all* illness, will help to convince you that this view is mistaken. Unfortunately the attitude of the public at large is unlikely to change very rapidly in this respect, despite the efforts of all concerned. Only when we can finally diagnose illnesses such as depression by means of an abnormal blood test or something similar will those who suffer from mood disorders be given the same degree of acceptance as those who have 'acceptable' problems such as angina or diabetes.

SEASONAL AFFECTIVE DISORDER (SAD)

As long ago as the 19th century there were reports from France of a variation in the frequency of psychiatric disorders and suicides with changes in the seasons.

Sufferers with this form of depression become ill when the days grow shorter and they are deprived of as much sunlight as they need. Many sufferers have found that taking holidays somewhere sunny in winter helps.

Symptoms of this disorder are similar to those of unipolar depressive episodes (*see* pages 6 and 7). There will be sleep disorders, in particular a tendency to want to sleep all the time. The feelings of depression will usually be at their worst in the afternoon and at night. Sufferers from SAD are, however, more likely than other depressives to have cravings for carbohydrate foods such as cakes, potatoes and chocolate, and are therefore likely to gain weight rather than lose it.

For depressive episodes to be classed as SAD in a person living north of the Equator, there has to be a regular appearance of the depressive symptoms between the beginning of October and the end of November. The patient will also completely recover, or change into a manic phase, between mid-February and mid-April.

Possible causes of this disorder and methods of treatment will be discussed in Chapters 4 and 7. It is of interest to note, however, that the desire to sleep for long periods and the craving for certain foods are not dissimilar to the quite natural behaviour of animals that hibernate during the winter months.

ANXIETY

On several occasions in the past few years I have had patients referred to me for treatment for panic attacks. On visiting them I have found a similar pattern. They tell me that they have experienced panic attacks in the past, but that they have invariably got better of their own accord. Now, however, the attacks have suddenly returned for no obvious reason.

People who suffer with panic attacks do tend to relapse during times of stress and then, once the stress is resolved, the panics go too – until the next time. In the cases in question I began treatment by instructing the patients how to overcome their panics, and practise certain relaxation techniques.[1]

Typically, at my next visit some three weeks later I would find that, despite the patient's very best efforts at doing what I had asked, the panics were no better. The patient would be encouraged to keep trying, possibly using different techniques. Another month or so would pass, until, at the third visit, about two months after the original referral, the picture would become clear. At this visit the patient would be obviously depressed, tearful, not sleeping well, experiencing thoughts of worthlessness, suicide etc. It now became obvious that these cases were not instances of panic attacks at all, but depressive episodes. Once treated with the right anti-depressant not only did the depression lift, but the panic attacks went away as well.

Depression may also be masked by anxiety in cases where sufferers feel helpless and unable to control their lives. (For more about the role played by helplessness, *see* Chapter 5.) I can best demonstrate this by relating the story of a problem a friend recently asked for advice with.

My friend works in the Housing Department of her local council. Her main task is to move people from council accommodation that has become unsuitable to somewhere more appropriate. Her problem arose when she had to get Mrs Johnson to move from a damp and draughty two-bedroomed house in the centre of town, to a more suitable modern one-bedroomed flat.

Mrs Johnson is a woman in her mid-forties who is unemployed. She has a grown-up son who no longer lives with her. She has been divorced twice. She has also regularly complained to various members of the Housing Department that she wants something done about the cold and damp in her home. When it was suggested that it might be better if she moved, she thought it a good idea. It was only when she was taken to inspect prospective flats that she became 'difficult'.

My friend was at her wits' end when she contacted me. Initially Mrs Johnson had agreed to move into a flat a couple of miles out of town on the edge of a large estate. She had insisted that the proposed flat should be refurbished before she would move. Apparently the surveyor had agreed to this and much money was spent on a new floor and redecoration. When the time came for Mrs Johnson to sign the agreement, however, she withdrew. My friend was at a loss to understand why.

Mrs Johnson refused to co-operate in any way and would not visit the Housing Department. She became agitated and tearful, and threatened suicide, when the matter was discussed. It was finally discovered that she was afraid she would lose her social life, such as it was, if she consented to move. She had no car and could not afford taxis to the pubs in town from her new home. She had been unable to voice this fear, however, and had become more and more depressed at the prospect. Her depression had come across as agitation, and been interpreted by others as anxiety. Those in the Housing Department had tended to view the change of mind as stubbornness and had become even less helpful towards her, which had made her feel even more threatened, less amenable, and more agitated as a result.

In the end my friend found a flat nearer town, one that was not as nice, but which suited Mrs Johnson. Thus it all ended happily.

POST TRAUMATIC STRESS DISORDER
(PTSD)

This disorder is not a depressive illness, but a sufferer may appear to be depressed in mood. It occurs after someone has been in a situation which most people would find extremely stressful. Examples of events which might provoke such a reaction are being the victim of violent crime, being involved in a major disaster or witnessing the violent death of others. The disorder usually starts within six months of the trauma which triggers it.

Symptoms include reliving the trauma in the form of dreams or 'flashbacks'. Apart from these symptoms, there are also insomnia, a lack of emotional expression and a tendency to avoid things which used to give pleasure – symptoms of depressive episodes. There may also be thoughts of suicide.

Other traumas, apparently quite mild, may also lead to depression, although they are not always classed as PTSD. Huni had come from Malaysia to work in the UK. He ran his own small supermarket. He was involved in a fairly minor accident while driving his car, when he was shunted into the rear of the car in front. As a result, he developed a phobia for driving. He still managed to make himself drive when he had to, but he no longer enjoyed it and was often anxious.

At the start of treatment he was very keen and determined to get the better of his symptoms. By the third session, in spite of trying very hard (probably too hard) to do what I advised, he was becoming despondent. At the fourth session he was obviously depressed. He complained of waking up early in the morning and being unable to get back to sleep. He said that if he relaxed at home to enjoy TV he fell asleep. He also said that he had lost interest in making himself try to get better even though, deep down, he still wanted to.

It seemed that he viewed his failure to prevent the accident, and the fact that he had then developed this fear which intruded on his enjoyment of life, as an indication that he could no longer control his own life. As the months had passed, this loss of confidence in himself had allowed him to drift into depression. We will be looking at the very close relationship between loss of confidence and depression again in Chapter 3.

Huni received anti-depressants which relieved his depression and left him able to do what was needed to overcome his driving phobia.

POSTNATAL DEPRESSION

As the name implies, this condition occurs up to six weeks after a woman has given birth. She becomes unduly tired, has sleep difficulties, is filled with despair, lacks confidence and loses her self-esteem.

Many mothers may say that with the problems of coping with a new baby it is surprising that all mothers do not suffer such symptoms. They may regard the fact that only about 20 to 25 per cent of mothers are affected as extremely low. However, postnatal depression is not thought to be quite the same as the 'baby blues' which affect the majority of women almost immediately after giving birth, when they swing in mood between feeling euphoric and tearful. 'Baby blues' are thought to be a direct result of the hormonal changes involved in the birth process.

Having had children of my own, I think they might also be triggered by social factors. At first the mother is relieved that the ordeal is over, and has a cute new little baby to get to know. Everyone wants to see it and she is proud to show it off. Then the novelty wears off. It ceases to be special, and the mother has to start doing tedious things again instead of sitting in bed being pampered. She has to cope with the demands of the infant as well as the lingering aches and pains in her own body. Is it any wonder the majority of women feel a bit depressed?

PUERPERAL PSYCHOSIS

This is the most severe form of depression associated with childbirth, and it only happens to about one woman in 1,000. It seems to be closely related to whatever causes bipolar depressive disorders since there is a far higher incidence of it in women who have already experienced a bipolar depression (one in ten).

The symptoms are similar to those which occur in severe forms of bipolar depression. The delusions, however, tend to centre on the new baby. The mother may believe it is deformed, the incarnation of evil or something similar and, because of her delusions, may try to harm either the baby or herself or both.

BEREAVEMENT

The sadness that is experienced at the time of a bereavement is not considered to be a form of depressive illness unless it is either more severe or continues for longer than might be expected given the normal social customs. When this happens, it becomes an adjustment disorder.

Other examples of adjustment disorders are distress and emotional disturbance relating to such life events as serious physical illness, loss of a job or homelessness.

BRAIN PATHOLOGY

When there has been damage to the brain as the result of an accident or disease, symptoms similar to those found in depressive disorders may result. The nature and severity of these obviously depends upon the site of the damage. It is often difficult to tell whether the symptoms indicate a depressive illness or are simply the result of brain damage. Sometimes there can be a depressive illness as well as brain damage, and it is important to recognize this so that the depression may be treated.

Alzheimer's disease, which occurs in the elderly and in which the brain deteriorates faster than normal, is one disorder in which symptoms similar to those found in depressive episodes are common.

Depressive illness is often overlooked in the elderly because many of the symptoms are simply put down to ageing and viewed as not treatable. Many elderly people have sleep difficulties, weight loss, and concentration and memory problems. Many also suffer from depression caused by a loss of self-esteem (more about this in Chapter 8).

DEPRESSIVE PERSONALITY

This condition is not an illness at all. It is a personality trait. A depressed mood is a personality state. So, what is the difference?

A personality trait is an aspect of your personality that remains more or less constant no matter what. It might be called a disposition. If, for instance, someone is said to be of a 'happy disposition', we understand this to mean that they react happily to most things most of the time. They may occasionally get sad, but only with justification. Thus, 'happy' here would be a personality trait.

In the same way, a person with a depressive personality trait will tend to see the down or negative side of almost everything almost all the time.

On the other hand, a personality *state* refers to a passing mood. If you suddenly feel happy because someone has given you a surprise gift, you are in a happy mood or personality state. It does not necessarily follow that you are of a happy disposition.

If you are sad because your dog has died, you are in a depressed state. Thus, a depressed state, or mood, is what people get when they have a depressive disorder. The depressive outlook is not a permanent feature of their personality.

Some people with depressive personalities do, however, also get depressive illnesses. It remains a matter of debate as to whether they are more susceptible to them than those of a happy disposition. Recent research that claims your thoughts affect your mood, and can even change the chemical balances within you, seems to suggest that this would tend to be the case.

CHAPTER 3

What Causes Depression?

When considering the causes of any form of depression there are three different aspects to take into account. First, who is most likely to get depressed (susceptibility)? Second, what will actually make them depressed (trigger)? Third, what keeps them feeling depressed (maintenance)?

SUSCEPTIBILITY

Who is most likely to become depressed? Not everyone with the same lifestyle and the same things happening to them will develop a depressive illness. The different forms of depression are not necessarily caused in the same way. Furthermore, the cause may not be the same as what keeps the disorder going. There are certain factors, known in medical language as predisposing factors, that make some people more likely to suffer from certain types of depression than others. So, what are they?

Sex

Statistics suggest that women are more likely to suffer from a depressive illness than men. Two out of three patients in hospitals with such disorders are women, and most of them are married. The proportions are the same among those seen by doctors but not admitted to hospital. There are suggestions that women born since the mid

1960s are showing signs of being slightly less likely to become depressed, although this has not yet been confirmed. But what does it imply?

Most women are aware that their own hormonal changes can make them more susceptible to mood changes around the time of their monthly period, during pregnancy, after childbirth and at the menopause. In some women this takes the form of varying degrees of irritability, in others it can induce melancholy.

If a woman is already suffering from a depressive illness, it may be exaggerated by these hormonal factors, but they alone do not cause the depression. Nevertheless they may be considered to be a predisposing factor. A woman may be more susceptible to a depressive illness, given other necessary factors, around the times of hormonal changes.

The other reason why more women suffer depressive illnesses than men seems to be due to the way society treats them, and its expectations of them. The fact that rates of depressive illness tend to change for entire generations suggests that it is an illness that is very strongly influenced by the social mores of the time.

As I have said, recent figures seem to indicate a reduction in women's susceptibility to depression. This may reflect their changing role in society and the general trend for them to be more involved in activities outside the home than previously. This hypothesis is supported by research[2] which showed that women were susceptible to depression if they lacked a full- or part-time job and were involved in the care of young children.

The reason for this is that women who have no job outside the home, or who have little time for themselves because of the demands of young children, tend to lose their sense of identity. They see themselves as people who are only there to serve the needs of others. This leads to a loss of self-esteem and self-confidence which, in turn, contributes to the feelings of unworthiness that are a common feature of depressive illnesses.

It has also been suggested that women confide more in their friends at work than men do. This freedom to confide can be a release and helps overcome any build-up of negative feelings and tensions before they have the chance to develop into a mood disorder. People cannot always express certain types of feeling to those who love them, for reasons examined in greater detail in Chapter 8.

Of course, men also suffer from depressive illnesses, and their susceptibility may also be due to social factors. One possible, though as yet unproven, reason for the apparent increase in the proportion of men suffering depression is that, as women's roles change, so men are becoming less sure of theirs. Whereas once a man was able to regard himself as head of the household and the main provider, women's recent reluctance to remain at home as subordinates has challenged this role. Men find that they are unable to assume the dominant position simply because they were born male. It is, perhaps, this insecurity which is making them more susceptible to depression.

A male friend of mine said recently that he believed all male depression was related to sexual difficulties. By this he did not mean problems with the sex act itself, but rather problems over close relationships of the type involving sex.

I disputed this at first. But on reflection and further discussion, I had to concede he had a point. I have explained this further in Chapter 10.

Other studies show that increased depression in men is closely linked to increases in alcoholism, drug abuse and suicide. Whether depression leads to alcoholism and drug abuse or vice versa not clear.

Heredity

Does depression run in families? Some forms do appear to be at least partly inherited. In this respect, susceptibility to depression seems to be like other inherited traits in that some people in the family inherit it and others do not. It might be concluded, therefore, that there is a genetic predisposition to some kinds of depression.

Close relatives of sufferers of severe bipolar depression are more likely to suffer from a unipolar or bipolar depression than others. One study has estimated that of people with no family history of bipolar or unipolar depression, only one in 100 will develop the bipolar kind and three in 100 will develop the unipolar kind. On the other hand, among those people who do have a family history of unipolar depression, one in ten will develop the disorder. If they have a family history of bipolar depression then one in five will develop it.

Studies[3] comparing identical twins (who have the same genes) with non-identical twins show that, of identical twins, 67 out of 100 will develop severe bipolar depression if their twin does. It makes little difference whether the twins are brought up together in the same environment or apart. Among non-identical twins, only 23 out of 100 will develop the disorder if their twin does.

Evidence such as this is pretty conclusive. A susceptibility to severe bipolar depression is genetically transmitted, but we do not yet know which genes are involved. It does not necessarily follow, however, that just because someone inherits the susceptibility, he or she will develop the illness.

Age

Apart from the close association between the menopause in women and a susceptibility to depression, there are other factors which have to do with the changes in lifestyle that occur as one gets older.

Elderly people are particularly susceptible to depression, especially if they lose their self-esteem. They may begin to see themselves as useless – a burden to society and their families. Their close friends may die before them. Loneliness and the loss of a purpose in life make the elderly more susceptible to depressed moods. Exactly how these lead on to a depressive illness is not certain, but we will discuss the possibilities in Chapter 8.

Environment

Certain types of everyday situation have been found to be closely associated with depressive illness.

It was found[4] that people who lost their mothers before the age of 11 and those who lacked a close relationship with someone they could confide in were more susceptible to depression.

I have already mentioned that married women form the largest group of people to suffer from depressive illnesses. This seems at first to be at odds with the finding that the lack of a close, confiding relationship can put someone more at risk of depression. Surely that is what married women have, so why do they become depressed more often than other groups?

The answer seems to be related to the type of marital relationship: a bad one is worse than none at all. I have already mentioned that low self-esteem is another factor that makes a person susceptible to depression. It is suggested that women with low self-esteem are more likely to marry unsuitable men because they are afraid that nobody else will want them. Hence these women not only lack close, confiding relationships, but their bad relationships on top of their lack of self-esteem make them very vulnerable to depressive illness.

Another environmental factor which can contribute to depression is poor living conditions. However, it is the way in which the person *thinks* about their predicament which is the biggest factor in the development of most forms of depression.

TRIGGERS

What causes a person who is susceptible to tip over the edge into a depressive illness? In most types of depression it is a stressful incident of some kind. Such an incident may not be regarded as stressful by others, but the important thing is that it causes stress to the person who is vulnerable. Even episodes of severe bipolar depression are thought by some to be triggered by stressful incidents.

Some depressive episodes seem to begin for no obvious reason, other than the fact that the person may have had a similar episode in the past. The sufferer is not always able to say what first caused him or her to feel low. It is thought that such episodes may be caused by some kind of biological or chemical change in the body which does not appear to be within the control of the sufferer.

They might be triggered by certain foods, by imbalances caused by hormonal changes, or even by changes in the sufferer's biochemistry brought about by the way he or she thinks and feels. In some cases they appear to be associated with stressful life events, but in others they do not. What is inherited may be an inability in some part of the body's system always to maintain the correct chemical balance, rather like the defective insulin production in diabetics.

The fact that depressions such as puerperal psychosis can sometimes be associated with hormonal changes supports the view that they are due to a bodily imbalance, but we do not yet know how it is triggered.

Some sufferers will say that their illness was triggered by events or changes in their life, usually involving some kind of loss or personal threat.

MAINTENANCE

In all but some of the most severe forms of depression, it is sufferers' reaction to the depression and their thoughts about the incidents that caused it which are often important for maintaining it.

It is therefore not so much the actual trigger for the depression which is most important, but knowing which factors are keeping it going, making it deeper. These factors may be considered under two headings: personality traits and environmental influences.

Personality Traits

A tendency to look on the negative side of things can be a maintenance factor in someone who is suffering from any degree of unipolar depression. If someone succumbs to a depressive illness and happens to have a depressive personality, as described at the end of Chapter 2, he or she is going to find it that much harder to get better. This is because thoughts appear able to influence the chemical balance within the human body. So, negative ways of thinking can keep depression going. There is more about this on pages 29 and 30.

Environmental Influences

These refer to the part played by the situations people find themselves in – their jobs, their homes, their relationships. If one of these is unsatisfactory in some way, it will make sufferers feel even worse, and it will be harder for them to think positively in order to help themselves get better. There is more about positive thinking in Chapter 9.

MIND–BODY RELATIONSHIP

This is perhaps the most important aspect of all psychological, and possibly physical, illness, yet most people ignore it completely. All too often we think of our bodies and our minds as totally separate entities. Unfortunately traditional medicine has tended to perpetuate this view in its obsession with treating only the sick part of the anatomy and paying the minimum of attention to the way the patient actually thinks or feels about what is happening.

I was listening to a radio programme the other day, in which a doctor was bemoaning the fact that the old-style convalescent homes no longer exist in the UK. In the 1950s and earlier, people who had major operations were discharged from hospital to spend some weeks recuperating in these homes and generally regaining their strength.

The doctor had recently had major surgery himself. In the spirit of efficiency and cost saving, he had been discharged from hospital only a few days after the operation in order to convalesce at home, having been told to take it easy. He found, to his cost, that although he tried to relax at home, it was not possible. There were constant interruptions, and people tried to involve him in aspects of his usual daily life when he could not really be bothered. Other members of the family banged doors and played loud music and he did not really feel he had the energy to do anything about stopping it.

Hence he finally returned to work with a healed body but feeling tense and stressed and more aware than he had been before of the need to pay attention to emotional needs in the treatment of physical illness.

We generally accept that if there is some kind of chemical change within our bodies, then our emotions and behaviour may be affected. What we have to begin to acknowledge is that the way we think, the expressions we have on our faces, and perhaps even the ways in which we move, may, in their turn, actually change the chemicals that are released inside us, and especially in our brains where our emotions are controlled.

In his book *Mega Brain Power*[5] Michael Hutchison suggests the following exercise. First note how you feel now. Next keep the left side of your face as still as you can and smile as hard as you can with the right side only. As you smile, make sure that the muscles in your cheek, lip and the side of your eye are all used. After a few moments stop and ask yourself if your mood has changed slightly.

What usually happens is that by working the muscles on the right side of the face you trigger positive emotions such as joy and light-heartedness. Had you worked the muscles of the left side you would have been more likely to experience negative emotions such as sadness.

This would seem to be due to the functions of the two sides (hemispheres) of the brain.

The brain, like the body, is made up of two sides. Each looks the same, but each holds special responsibility for certain functions. For example, the left side of the brain controls the right side of the body, and vice versa. Therefore, when you exercise the muscles of the right side of your face, you are working with the left side of your brain.

Various researchers have compared the brain waves of their subjects, recorded by means of an electroencephalograph (EEG) machine, with their personalities. They have found that those who have high electrical activity in the left frontal areas of the brain also tend to be of a cheerful disposition. On the other hand, those who have more activity in the right frontal areas tend to be sad and to see the world in more negative terms.

We must realize that our minds and bodies work together, each affecting the other. The experiment of working the muscles of one side of your face and feeling the effects on your emotions should convince you. If not, remember the last time you were afraid of something. Did your heart not beat faster, your mouth go dry, your palms perhaps become clammy, your attention focus only on what you were afraid of? All these physical reactions only came about because you thought 'fear'. Had you been asleep at the time you came into contact with what it was that made you feel afraid, you would not have experienced any of those symptoms.

It is what you think that generally triggers your emotions. Unfortunately, we rarely think, 'I'm happy' unless circumstances are so wonderful that we cannot ignore them. If only we could learn to see the positive, good side of our lives more often!

There is a great deal of research currently being undertaken into the effects of our thoughts on our brains and the chemicals produced. It is highly likely that in the second decade of the 21st century we will look back at the way in which we now treat our minds and bodies as two separate entities and it will seem prehistoric. Current thinking, however, is that depressive illness is triggered by a bodily imbalance of some kind, and it will not improve until that imbalance is corrected. This is usually achieved with anti-depressant drugs.

YOUR THOUGHTS

The final, and possibly the most influential factor in depressive illness is one's own way of thinking about what is happening to one. People with a depressive personality, as described at the end of Chapter 2, will find it more difficult to overcome depression because of their habit of thinking negatively and looking on the black side. This will tend to create in them that very chemistry which leads to depression.

I have already mentioned that low self-esteem can make you susceptible to depression. But what is low self-esteem? In brief it is the feeling that one does not deserve anything, that one is not as important as others. It is felt by people who have always been made or expected to put others first.

A person with low self-esteem tends to think that their wishes and feelings are less important than those of the people around them. For various reasons, they have lost the ability to put themselves first, if they ever had it. They have no idea of how they would feel or act if left to their own devices, because their lives are almost totally laid out for them by the needs of others.

Mothers of young children and carers of the elderly or disabled are often victims of low self-esteem. They very often get along without even realizing that they are doormats. Problems only arise when they find themselves confronted by a choice between what they suddenly discover they really want, and their 'duty'. They feel guilty at discovering that they have wants that can only be fulfilled at some cost to those for whom they are caring.

At such times they become aware that as a consequence of putting others first they have lost their self-identity without realizing it. They now feel unimportant, disregarded. When they try to tell those closest to them how they feel, their feelings and protests are brushed aside. Many a husband has told his wife, at home all day with small children, that she has nothing to complain about when all she has to do is sit around drinking tea with her friends! Such is the breeding ground for depression.

Because they have not been in the habit of having their own needs considered, when they become depressed they tend to accept it as just what worthless people like them deserve, and they become powerless to help themselves. This is the vicious downward depressive spiral which has to be broken. Until it is, the sufferer is in an emotional prison. It is the hardest of all to break out of – but it is not impossible.

CHAPTER 4

The Body and Depression

Now let us look at some of the mechanisms of the body and consider how these might one day be shown to be involved in depressive disorders. Some of the evidence is still very flimsy, but it is often from what appear initially to be strange ideas that good research develops.

HORMONES

This seems the obvious place to start in view of the fact that women become depressed more often than men, and most women know that they tend to feel low just before a period. We saw in Chapter 2, that there is a particular form of severe depressive disorder that occurs after child-birth – puerperal psychosis. We also know that the vary-ing mood which a majority of women get immediately after giving birth – 'baby blues' – is thought to be triggered by hormonal changes, as is the other form of depressive disorder that occurs around this time, post-natal depression.

The fact that these depressive disorders are closely linked with hormonal changes does not account for the vast majority of depressions, but in how great a propor-tion does it play a significant part? Is hormonal disruption a trigger for something else to happen, which then causes the depression in vulnerable people?

Mental illness of any kind, as I said in the context of CFS (*see* page 12), is regarded as a weakness, something that the sufferer should not have allowed to develop. Physical illness, on the other hand, because it is widely regarded as being no fault of the sufferer, is seen as acceptable, if unfortunate. But things are changing.

In the past it seems that, because our society expected men to show a 'stiff upper lip' and not make a fuss, they tended to try and disregard any emotional problems. With the 'new man' and our acknowledgement that men have feelings too, they are beginning to dare to admit to more of these. Therefore, the fact that statistics have always shown women to suffer more from various depressive and anxiety disorders may not mean that women are more likely to suffer from them, but rather that they are more likely to admit that they have them.

Last week the husband of one of my patients told me that, in his opinion, men could even have hormonal problems, just as women do. He related how, when he was in his late teens, he and three of his friends all experienced depressive episodes for no reason that they could fathom. At the time they supported one another because they felt it was unmanly to seek help, and after several months it sorted itself out.

When the effects of the normal monthly cycle in women have been closely studied, no direct relationship has been found between it and depression. In other words, one does not lead to the other. On the other hand, the two do sometimes tend to go together. It is feasible, then, that hormonal changes make a person susceptible to depressive feelings, but do not cause them.

It is thought that there is probably a direct link between severe bipolar depression, featuring psychotic symptoms, and hormonal changes – as in puerperal psychosis. There is no evidence, however, that the other forms of depression are directly caused by hormonal changes.

Some diseases where there is known to be a problem with correct hormone control, such as thyroid disorders, also tend to feature symptoms of depression. Thus it seems that incorrectly balanced hormone function is related to depression, but whether it can actually cause the depression is another matter.

NEUROTRANSMITTERS

In order to function, our entire system relies on messages being transmitted from the brain to the various parts of the body and back again. If you want to move your little toe, there has to be a message of intent sent from your brain to tell the toe to move. There are also other transmissions that tell you it is moving and how it is moving. If you see something that makes you sad, there have to be messages that relay what you see with your eyes to your brain, which makes sense of the pictures, decides what it thinks, then issues the appropriate instructions for how you are to feel.

There is a great debate as to whether, in disorders such as depression, it is the brain telling you to be sad that causes the depression, or whether something in your body tells your brain that it must feel sad. In other words, does the trigger for the disorder come from your thoughts to your body, or the other way round?

It has long been argued that to treat a mood disorder such as depression with drugs is to assume that the trigger is coming *from* the body *to* the thoughts. Those who say they are depressed because of what they are thinking, would tend to seek the solution in changing their thoughts, with talking therapy of some kind, and then hope that their bodily feelings would follow suit.

In fact it seems that it is not strictly a case of one or the other. It would appear that although bodily changes can affect your thoughts, your thoughts can also cause changes in your body. The old idea that a good laugh would do you good is not so ridiculous. Remember the experiment where you screwed up one side of your face and possibly felt your mood change ever so slightly for the better or worse as a result? It is the same principle – if you laugh, that laughter and the muscles involved can send good messages to your brain which can then adjust the body for the good.

Unfortunately we do not know how or why this happens just yet so one cannot have a prescription for six episodes of *Fawlty Towers* to cure the flu – although if one enjoys *Fawlty Towers* it can only help. There is an old saying, 'A little of what you fancy does you good.' People may not have known how or why many of their remedies worked in the old days, but they were often more right than we are today, for all our scientific advances.

Neurotransmitters are the chemicals that help to send the messages to and from the brain. I will only describe how they work very briefly here; if you want more detail, I would suggest that you consult a biology textbook. What happens is that electrical impulses carrying the messages are passed through the body along the nerves, from one nerve cell to another. The nerve cells are called neurones. Between one neurone and the next, however, there is a gap called a synapse. The impulse has to jump this gap to carry on. When it reaches the gap neurotransmitters are released, so allowing the message to cross.

It is a little like electricity being conducted across a gap through water. Water carries electricity well and if two things are connected by a little moisture, an electric current will cross more easily between them. The neurochemicals are like the water in this respect; they make it possible for the impulse containing the message to cross the gap. There must also be another neurochemical, called a receptor, on the other side of the gap to receive the message.

After a neurochemical has done its work, it has to be reabsorbed by the body. This is why exercise is beneficial to anxious people. Anxiety messages stimulate a particular chemical so that they can cross the gaps. Exercise rids the body of these neurotransmitter chemicals when they have done their job. Exercise thus helps control anxiety. It has also been found to be useful in depression – more about that in Chapter 9.

If the wrong neurotransmitters are being produced to bridge these gaps, or incompatible receptors are meeting them, then the body works inefficiently in some way and illness results. It is this that is the theory behind the belief that many psychiatric illnesses, especially depression, may one day be shown to be due to just such a defect. Once the imbalance is identified, then steps can be taken to correct it and the problem will be cured.

Many of the anti-depressants that are used, and that have been used for many years, are made up of substances designed to correct the imbalances that are thought to exist. The fact that they sometimes work and sometimes do not implies that one has to treat the imbalance with the right drug for that person. Moreover, with a disorder so closely tied in with one's thoughts and feelings, it is possible that other factors in the sufferer's life are causing the imbalance to continue in spite of all attempts to balance it out with drugs. These other factors would need to be found and corrected too. Chapter 7 explains how this is done at present. Methods of treatment are much better than they were, and are getting better all the time.

CIRCADIAN RHYTHMS

Circadian rhythms are the cycles by which we live day in day out: getting up, eating, working, playing, then going to sleep again. Our entire bodily system is usually adapted to the rhythm so that, when we are well and living normally, we feel hungry, tired, etc at the right time.

Experiments, in which subjects have been isolated from any means of telling the time, have shown that their rhythms will still follow more or less their usual pattern.[6] It is thought that light and darkness may play a part in keeping the rhythm going. It has been suggested that people who suffer from SAD have a delay in their circadian rhythm and that extra light, in the form of a holiday in the sun or special artificial lights, advances the rhythm and gets it back to normal. Why it slows down in the first place is not known.

One of the stages of sleep is REM which stands for rapid eye movement. It can easily be seen by someone watching the sleeper because the eyes move rapidly under the eyelids, and it is the stage of sleep when dreams occur. Normally when we fall asleep, we spend some time in shallow sleep, progress into REM, then go deeper. As we then come out of this deep sleep again we go through another phase of REM. This cycle repeats itself about four times a night, with REM sleep occurring about every hour and a half. If people are not permitted to have REM sleep they develop hallucinations, usually seeing and sometimes hearing things that do not exist. It seems that we need our REM sleep and our dreams, whether we remember them or not.

It has been found that REM occurs more frequently in depression. It has also been found, however, that if depressed patients are deprived of sleep, they improve, but relapse again after sleeping. The best effects occur if patients are not allowed to sleep during the second part of the night. This is not surprising since, if depressed people try to follow a normal routine, they tend to wake up in the early hours anyway and be unable to go back to sleep. It has been found that the depression improves if they bring their sleep period forward by about six hours. So if they normally go to bed at 10pm, they would go at 4pm, and get up at 1am instead of 7am.

In depression, a number of circadian rhythms appear to be out of step, especially the sleep cycle which tends to end earlier than normal, as we have seen. Some researchers argue that the key to the causes of depression lies in the disruption of the circadian rhythms.[7] They say that defects in the neurotransmitters cannot account for all the symptoms, although a defect of the body clock can. Moreover, anti-depressant drugs do, in fact, work on circadian rhythms to lift depressive symptoms.

Anyone who has had their 'body clock' severely

disrupted will know how dreadful it can make one feel. Jet lag is a case in point. It is thought to be caused by the disturbance of sleep patterns. It is said to be worse when travelling from east to west. Flying east to west is more likely to make you depressed if you are that way inclined, while flying from west to east is more likely to produce feelings of mania. So if someone flies east, they are more likely to feel happy when they arrive and low when they return. Such mood changes are not likely to be great enough to be noticed by most people, however, because they generally feel simply exhausted after sitting with their knees in their chests in a tiny aeroplane seat for hours!

BRAIN WAVES

Studies of changes in EEG activity in the different parts of the brain of depressed people have shown some interesting findings.

The EEG is a means of recording brain activity that has been around for many years, and it is quite painless. Electrodes are placed at certain points on the head and the patient is asked to relax, watch a flickering light or close their eyes. The electrodes record the brain waves in the different parts of the brain.

As we have seen, our brains have two sides, known as hemispheres. In most people, the left hemisphere is regarded as the dominant one. This side of the brain is responsible for logical thought, for mental calculations, for putting things in order. It is also the side through which we think in terms of words. The right hemisphere, regarded as the non-dominant one in most people, is the side that deals with images, creativity and the more artistic side of life.

There is much evidence to suggest that people who suffer from manic depression – ie severe recurrent bipolar depression – are often also very creative, including people such as Spike Milligan the entertainer, and Robert Schumann the composer.

So which part of the brain is involved? The exercise outlined on pages 27–8, which involved contorting one side of your face, produced sadder feelings when done to the left side. This side is controlled by the right hemisphere of the brain, which is associated with creativity. And creativity is loosely associated with bipolar depression.

Several studies have found that people with high levels of activity in the front regions of the left hemisphere have a more cheerful and positive outlook. They have been found to be more self-confident, outgoing and happy. People whose EEG tests show more activity in the front areas of the right hemisphere are more negative in their outlook. They tend to see the worst side of things and blame themselves more.

It appears to be best to have equal amounts of activity in each hemisphere – known as brain symmetry. Another study[8] found that people who had just been diagnosed as suffering from depression had less left front activity than people who were not depressed. In other words, it is not only more activity than normal in the right side that makes someone liable to become depressed, but also less activity than normal in the left side, thus making the two sides unbalanced.

The relevance of these findings for future treatment methods will be discussed later. It seems, however, that this imbalance in the activity of this part of the brain may be inherited since its effects have been found in babies.

THE IMMUNE SYSTEM

The immune system – the system which the body calls upon to defend it against invasion by infection or anything else that does not belong – is one part of our bodily functioning which has been found to be controllable by our thoughts. It can be affected by hypnosis, by meditation and by one's outlook on life. It has been found that in depression the body's immune system does not function as well as usual. Experiments with groups of subjects who were measured as being stressed showed that they had a reduced ability to reject foreign matter in their bodies, and to fight infection.

In short, it is thought that if we adopt a positive approach to life and look on the bright side, we will help our immune system cope, and will be less likely to fall prey to all kinds of infections, from viruses to cancers. Everyone has heard of people who have overcome cancer, people such as my friend's mother. She was diagnosed as having cancer in 1947 and expected to live no longer than a year. But she decided that she did not have time for cancer and, still untreated, lived until 1983.

On the other hand, if a person wants to die or believes death is inevitable, then the immune system will weaken and they will die. There are many examples quoted by anthropologists of tribes in Africa where a man has been told by the witch doctor that he will die, often for some misdemeanour. In a few weeks this perfectly fit and healthy man will be dead because he believed he would be!

There are also many instances of elderly couples where one partner dies and the survivor simply loses the will to continue living alone. A few months after the first death, the surviving partner succumbs to a viral infection, such as pneumonia, and dies as well.

CHAPTER 5

How Does it Feel to be Depressed?

Sadness is unpleasant but it is not as bad as depression. When people are sad, they keep their self-respect, they feel better for a good cry, they confide in others and it helps. When they are depressed their self-respect fades, crying does not help at all, even if they can manage to do it, and they feel alienated because other people cannot seem to understand how they feel and they do not have the energy or the will to explain.

To become depressed is to feel as if one is falling into a huge black hole of nothing. When a depression comes on slowly, for no obvious reason, this feeling can be so slow that one has the sensation of watching it happen. Sufferers feel themselves getting nearer and nearer to the black hole. Like a spider in the bath being flushed down a plug hole, they feel their world spinning more and more out of control. They spin faster and faster as they get closer and closer to the hole.

Then, all at once, they are falling down into it and nothing seems the same as it was before. They really feel as if someone has turned the world upside down. Things do not appear as they did before, nor do they feel about them as they did.

They struggle for a while because they cannot believe that it is really happening. They try to make some sense of things, find some way out again, to climb back up the overflow like the spider and back into the bath. Sometimes, like the spider, they manage it. But then, something comes along and flushes them back down.

Some people will climb back up that overflow pipe several times. Some will manage to escape once they get back into the bath – they will find an answer and get out of the depression. Others, however, will just keep being washed back down. The worst part is that each time they make it back into the bath, they feel a tiny bit of hope creeping into their minds, hope that maybe this time they will be all right. Then they are washed back down, the hope dies a little, until finally it gives up altogether and refuses to grow any more. This state of hopelessness is the bleakest of all.

People's ability to bounce back differs. Depressed people have often already had to bounce back more times than most. Then suddenly they cannot do it any more. It is like the alcohol binges one may have had when young; eventually one tends to remember the hangover *before* one gets drunk, and thinks twice.

A patient once wrote the following for me about how she felt when she was very severely depressed:

> Things you used to care about, you can no longer be bothered with. If you were once house-proud, you feel you ought to care about doing the dusting – but you can't. No matter how much you try to persuade yourself it matters – it doesn't.
>
> You'd like to kill yourself and end it all, but your loved ones won't let you. You almost wish for some terminal disease so you could give up the struggle and escape without feeling guilty about hurting those you loved.
>
> Overall you're tired and lethargic. You go to bed early because you're bored. You wake up early but you have no desire to make the most of the day ahead. The day holds no promise, there's nothing you can't wait to do.
>
> You'll do anything to avoid feeling. You're so worn out by feeling – desperate, powerless, alone. You just don't want to care about anything because caring is feeling. If you feel you'll get hurt. You're thus quite happy to abandon the good in life.

Those who have never experienced an episode of clinical depression cannot imagine the total numbing of the feelings, nor even the complete lack of desire to be involved in anything pleasurable. We think we can, but only those who have truly been depressed are aware of the real difference.

This was brought home to me a few years ago by Jane, a married woman of 52. She had raised three children, two from her husband's previous marriage and one of her own. She had worked as a personnel manager before marrying. She had remained employed a little after her marriage, but when she had her daughter she found it just too much to cope with everything at once. Her husband had a very good job and, since they did not need the money, Jane gave up her career.

The years had passed happily enough. She had taken part in local activities, had done some courses in modern languages at night school, and had generally been content. Then all at once she found that all her children had left home and there was a gap in her life. She gave me the following example of how it is possible not to want even that which one has longed for.

She recounted the big scene in the TV adaptation of Colleen McCullough's *Thornbirds*[9] where Meggie, having had a disastrous marriage on the rebound, and having recently given birth to a daughter, is worn out and seemingly depressed. Her kind employers send her away to a holiday home on an island to recuperate.

Meggie has been in love almost all her life with Ralph, a Catholic priest. Ralph was put in charge of Meggie's inheritance because she was only a child at the time. He watched her grow up and we have the impression that he was more than fond of her, but was not going to break his vows of celibacy. Thus there were numerous scenes where the two of them yearned for one another but nothing happened.

Then, when Meggie is alone on the island, at her lowest emotional ebb, she takes a walk along the edge of the sea and, all at once, better than her wildest dreams, Ralph arrives.

How would one react in those circumstances? Most people would, I believe, seize the chance of happiness. But Meggie does not. She looks anguished, calls out something to the effect of, 'No, not again!' and runs away from him – leaving the viewer a mass of seething incomprehension and frustration. This is what depression does.

As Jane pointed out, in depression, one reaches a point where, even though one has lost all hope, in a strange way one finds relief. Suddenly all the torments and anguish cease because one loses both the desire and the ability to seek pleasure. In that state, as with Meggie, one even becomes afraid of pleasure, in case it starts one feeling again.

THE VICIOUS CYCLE

As we saw in Chapter 4, we are beginning to identify biological markers for depressive disorders, but we still do not know why they happen. Is it sad thoughts which cause the body to become imbalanced in some way or does the imbalance come first and cause the sad thoughts? This is still the big question.

Whatever the answer, since anti-depressants do work to lift depressions, it seems that correcting the body's imbalance can allow the sufferer to have positive thoughts once more. But do anti-depressants simply mask the thoughts and drown out the problem, only for it to come back later? If the cause of the problem is something in the sufferer's life, then this is likely to be the case. But how does one try and change the thinking of someone who has drifted into hopelessness and no longer cares?

This is the dilemma for the treatment of depression. Whatever triggers it, there are knock-on effects: negative thoughts lead to bodily changes which incline the sufferer to more negative thoughts, which in turn lead to more bodily changes. This is a vicious cycle that has to be broken before the depression will lift.

Trying to reason with or to talk a depressed person who has reached hopelessness is like typing on a computer keyboard when the system is 'hanging'. None of the keys you press has any effect whatsoever on the screen or the machine, other than perhaps the occasional angry bleep that seems to be saying, 'Leave me alone!'

HELPLESSNESS AND HOPELESSNESS

How do we come to feel helpless? It happens when our behaviour in response to something unpleasant proves pointless. Let us take the example of a good, careful driver. This person drives competently, not idiotically fast, but not too slowly either. He or she does not drive after drinking, keeps the right distance behind other cars, especially in the wet, and does not jump traffic lights.

Then, suddenly, one day when driving along a motorway, a tyre bursts on a lorry travelling in the inside lane causing it to swerve across the other two carriageways. Our driver sees it happen and manages to stop in time to avoid hitting it as it crosses in front. But the car behind does not.

After an accident like this, such a driver often begins to avoid motorways, feels anxious when driving, drives far more slowly than before, obsessively watches every other car on the road to attempt to guess what it is going to do next. This driver has experienced 'learned helplessness' in relation to driving – the realization that no matter what action one takes, and however careful one is, one cannot avoid unpleasant consequences.

When this happens with more major trauma, the disorder known as post traumatic stress disorder (PTSD) (*see* Chapter 2) often results. Sufferers lose confidence in themselves because they feel that their inability to do anything is a reflection on the rest of their abilities too. Depression is a feature of PTSD.

When people repeatedly find in their everyday life that

being good, honest, careful, loving and hard-working does not bring the results they expect – being loved, successful, happy, etc – they begin to lose confidence in themselves. They learn that behaving in a way that they have been brought up to believe is right does not avoid heartache. They feel helpless because their method has been proved ineffective, and they do not know what to do to get the results they want. So they give up, they feel helpless, they do nothing, they lapse into depression.

Helplessness usually happens when life repeatedly fails to live up to our expectations of it, or when we fail to control our environment as we want. A consequence of this feeling is that, within the body, that part of the immune system that normally fights disease and rebuilds tissue becomes less effective. In other words, a sense of helplessness can make one more vulnerable to physical disease.

A feeling of helplessness in one's job can also lead to an anxiety state or depression. A typical situation occurs when people are told that they have the power to make certain decisions, but find, time and again, that after they have worked hard and made those decisions, someone higher up brushes them aside and implements something completely different. This, not unnaturally, leads them to believe that their work is a waste of time. If they can move to another job they probably will. Unfortunately this is not an option for many people. They end up contracting all kinds of minor illnesses, no doubt brought about by their lowered resistance to infection because their immune systems are reacting to the sense of helplessness.

A popular concept in business at present is empowerment. This means that if someone is given responsibility for something their decisions in that matter should be respected. Therefore, in this context, empowerment means that people can believe that their actions will produce results, rather being steam-rollered by someone else's. Everyone needs to have a sense of real purpose – to feel that their actions do have some significance and are not just a time-wasting exercise. People who constantly feel that their life has no real purpose are at great risk of depressive disorders, and we will be discussing how this problem can be overcome in Chapter 9.

But there is a worse problem than helplessness, and that is hopelessness. Whereas the person feeling helpless will still tend to expect someone to come up with an answer that will show them how to cope with their predicament, the hopeless person has stopped believing that there is an answer that will suit the situation. The hopeless person may come up with several possible answers, but find that none of them are acceptable for various reasons.

People in a state of hopelessness have no way out at all; they do not feel in charge of their own life, or their feelings. Dorothy Rowe[10] talks of hopelessness as being in one's own private prison. The hopeless person is absolutely certain that there is no answer.

One can feel helpless without feeling hopeless, but one always feels helpless before feeling hopeless.

VULNERABLE LIFE POINTS

There are certain situations in life that cause more problems than others. The first of these is adolescence. Children first begin to have a real sense of their own identities around this time and so begin to be vulnerable to helplessness. Younger children, who are not accustomed to exerting a great deal of control over their environments, do not worry so much.

Many people who feel hopeless have suffered a form of emotional blackmail from those who love them. Take children whose parents expect great things of them. Perhaps the parents wanted to go to university but, for various reasons, never made it. They may be unduly keen for their children to go, thinking that it is the best start that anyone could have. The children, however, may not be very academically minded, and may find school work difficult. However, since they love their parents and know that they only want what is best, they try very hard.

But in spite of their efforts they may keep getting grades that are not quite good enough. The parents keep encouraging them, telling them that they are sure they will do well. They may even use all their spare money to pay for extra tuition for the children outside school hours. The children, knowing the sacrifices their parents are making, still try, but still do not succeed.

Finally they will develop a sense of hopelessness because nothing they do is ever quite good enough. They try to tell the parents they do not want to go to university. The parents become angry and accuse them of ingratitude after all they have done. Some children will then become rebellious and drop out. Others will be consumed by a sense of anger, guilt and frustration which will eventually turn to hopelessness. Such children may attempt suicide because they can see no other way out. They cannot do what is expected of them, they cannot get their parents to accept the problem, and they cannot rebel because they love their parents and that would hurt them.

Another problem children face is bullying. Children who are bullied at school will become afraid. They will not dare tell their parents because they are afraid the parents will go to the school and make a fuss; the other children will then find out and they will be bullied even more. They may try telling someone in authority, but this may not have a severe enough effect on the bullies. So they live in constant fear and anxiety until they, too, feel hopeless.

Sometimes a parent can let us down badly when we trust them. Take the case of Audrey. Her case goes back to the 1950s, but the type of emotional blackmail she suffered still happens today, although the situation may differ slightly.

Audrey was engaged to be married to Colin. The wedding was arranged, invitations were sent out, the church was booked. Suddenly Audrey realized that she didn't love Colin. She spent many hours in soul-searching and wondering if it mattered. She tried to tell herself that love was not essential – but she could not persuade herself. As the dreaded day drew nearer, Audrey became more and more depressed.

It did not help that both her own and Colin's mother talked of nothing else. They were so excited. Audrey dared once or twice to consider the consequences of calling it off, but felt so sorry for the disappointment she would cause the two mothers that she did not dare. As her sense of helplessness increased, so she became uninterested in the preparations. She was unable to sleep, and disinclined to eat, and she became ratty when she was with Colin. Finally her mother noticed her distress and begged Audrey to tell her what was wrong.

Audrey was tempted to tell her the truth, but decided against it. A few more days passed. Audrey's mother begged her again to confide in her. Audrey again felt that she could not. This went on for some time until, finally, two days before the wedding, she couldn't face her impending future any longer. She could not cope with everyone expecting her to be radiant and happy when she felt a big empty chasm inside.

The next time her mother asked what was wrong, begged Audrey to trust her and said it could be worked out whatever it was, Audrey took her at her word. She said, 'I don't want to marry Colin,' and waited. She discovered that she had been right about her mother's reaction. She immediately grew frantic, muttering about what people would think, the fact that they had already paid the caterers, how they would have to send back all the presents. Audrey recalls watching all this with a certain detachment because she had never expected to find a way out, and now her mother had proved it. She relented and said it was only pre-wedding nerves, that of course she would marry Colin. Her mother was instantly reassured; Audrey had said what she had wanted to hear, and all was well.

Audrey told me how she had stood in church making

her vows and asking God for forgiveness because she did not mean them. Soon after the wedding she sank into a still deeper state of hopelessness that took many months in hospital to resolve. Colin later left her for another woman.

Others become depressed when they suddenly discover that there is more to life than they have come to believe. They glimpse what I call 'scraps of untainted sky,' and are unable to ignore it. This term comes from E M Forster's story 'The Machine Stops'.[11]

The story concerns a time in the future when mankind is forced to live in a synthetic environment beneath the Earth's surface because the surface is too polluted. Everything in people's lives is controlled for them: whether they reproduce, what they do. They never walk so they are losing their legs; nature is evolving.

One day a rebel comes along – which is unusual because people are genetically engineered. One day this rebel finds out that there is something outside their world, on the surface. He goes there and returns. The story ends with an explosion and the one below sees 'scraps of the untainted sky'.

The thing is that once they have become aware of something wonderful outside their world, they cannot ignore it. You cannot ever go back to not knowing once you know something, however much you may want to. Adam and Eve found that out when they tasted the apple.

People sometimes see their 'scrap of untainted sky' when their lives are drifting along, giving them neither highs nor lows. All at once something happens which feels as if it has brought them alive once more. They suddenly realize that they are getting older and this is the only life they are going to have. They have financial responsibilities towards a spouse and perhaps even dependent children, who have supported them in their endeavours so far and who do not deserve to be abandoned. They find that they have to make a choice: to forget what they have seen and carry on as before, or to be brave and take a plunge into the unknown.

Many people become depressed when they recognize that they really want to take the plunge, but cannot hurt those who rely on them. They are riddled with guilt about what to do.

Some people come to terms with this and give up, making the most of what is allowed. Others cannot do so Perhaps they do not feel that they have achieved anything very significant in their lives.

The resentment grows. They may decide to give up and give in, but the determination does not last and they find themselves wishing they could break free. They feel out of control of their lives, tied by the emotions of others. They become depressed. Loved ones ask what is wrong, but they can't possibly say.

Sometimes this depression turns to hopelessness. Nicholas took a year out of what had, up to then, been a successful career as a merchant banker. He took out some of his investments in order to travel rough around the world with a group of like-minded people who had advertised the adventure in a magazine. His wife and two teenage children were a bit bemused by the sudden wanderlust but attributed it to a kind of male menopause and encouraged him to go.

It was the experience of a lifetime. Nicholas found himself truly free. Here he was no longer tied to the conventions and behaviour expected of him at home. He saw his other life as a sham, a pretence. On the last part of the voyage, as the group headed for home, Nicholas was unable to come to terms with going back. Although he loved his wife and children, he could not face their expectations of him – expectations he no longer felt able to fulfil. On the other hand he felt mean when he considered how supportive and encouraging they had been.

Over the last few weeks he became more and more confused about his feelings. He could not go back, but nor could he bear to hurt his family. He began to feel useless and a failure. In the end he despaired. As he lapsed into depression, his thinking grew more and more irrational and he felt more and more pressurized. He talked to no one about it because he felt guilty at having such thoughts.

In the end he died after falling from a mountain. He left behind tragically disjointed ramblings in a diary which helped to show how his depressive illness had evolved and explained his final act.

Although we regard it as abnormal to want to kill oneself, since all our instincts are towards survival at any cost, those who seriously consider it would argue that they know perfectly well what they are doing and that there is just no viable alternative. Life in its present state is intolerably bleak and they can see no hope of any other way out.

Suicide is often a very difficult concept for most people to come to terms with. But it happens. The next chapter is devoted to it.

CHAPTER 6

Suicide

Suicide is not an easy subject to write about, but to omit it from a book about depression would be wrong. If you have experience of suicide and you still feel anger or guilt about it, you should seek professional help to resolve the problem. This is a very serious aspect of depression and one which does not readily lend itself to self-help techniques.

Nevertheless, this chapter aims to explain some aspects of it to those who may be caring for someone who is depressed, and to help increase their awareness of potential suicide. This chapter is not written for those who feel suicidal themselves, but they're not likely to want to read it anyway.

There are 200,000 attempted suicides every year in the UK. A report from the Health Advisory Service in 1994, giving guidance on suicide prevention, stated that in 1992 there were more deaths from suicide in England and Wales (5,542) than from road accidents (3,814). The report said that health-care professionals should take prospective suicide cases more seriously and actively encourage the will to live.

There are people who threaten to commit suicide and there are people who make no threats and just do it. Both kinds must be taken seriously.

Those who threaten suicide are asking for help. They are telling us that as far as they can see, all ways out of their current predicament are barred to them. They are asking for help to make something possible. What they are not doing is simply trying to gain attention for its own sake.

The previous chapter explained, for the benefit of those fortunate enough never to have experienced the devastating feelings of deep depression, what it feels like and how it distorts one's perception of the world and one's place in it. With this knowledge, it is possible to see how, to the sufferers, suicide may seem the only possible way out of their predicament.

Fortunately, although those who are deeply depressed may be attracted by the relief of suicide, they generally lack the drive to do anything about putting their desires into practice. Deep depression leads some people to believe that they are so unworthy that they do not deserve to escape that way, that they deserve to go on suffering.

Ironically, as their condition seems to improve, some of them find the strength they needed. Their loved ones are left very confused because they had thought the person was getting better.

Those who are really determined to commit suicide will not tell anyone of their plans for fear of being thwarted. Those who are really determined, who really no longer wish to live, will find a way to succeed.

There was an interview on TV recently with a woman whose only son had been killed. This woman had no other relatives, no husband. Her son had been her whole life. She explained that as far as she was concerned, there was simply nothing left to live for. She had attempted suicide but, by pure chance, had been found and revived. In common with many people who truly see no point in living, however, she was not pleased to be alive and vowed not to be found the next time. She was quite rational, not unduly upset or obviously depressed. She explained that as far as she was concerned the option of taking her own life was one she ought to be allowed.

This woman had, as far as she could see, lost her only reason to live – her son. She had nothing left to live for.

Such decisions taken when suffering from depression would indeed seem to be the work of unbalanced minds.

It has already been stated that feelings of low self-esteem and worthlessness go hand in hand with depression. Those whose lives are restricted in activities and relationships are more at risk of depression and suicide than those whose lives are fuller. Suicide is most common following a bereavement. It is also relatively common in elderly men who, because they no longer work or have anyone to support, feel they've lost their purpose in life. Elderly men are also more likely than women to commit suicide when suffering severe physical illness.

People with certain jobs have been shown to have higher rates of suicide than others. Doctors are known to be one such group. In this case the stresses of their work have always been cited as a viable reason for the above average numbers of doctors who commit suicide.

Two other groups have high rates: vets and farmers. This statistic defied satisfactory explanation until recently. It has been suggested that a viral infection, which humans can contract from certain farm animals, may lead them, when infected, to become severely depressed to a sometimes suicidal degree. This hypothesis makes sense. We know that viral infections, such as flu, often leave us feeling a bit low, sometimes even depressed. It is not inconceivable, then, that some infections bring abut more severe depressive illnesses than others. However, this hypothesis has not yet been finally tested.

Whatever the truth, those of us who suspect someone is contemplating suicide will do all we can to prevent them, in the belief that they will be glad to be still alive one day. Those who are really determined, however, will take care not to let anyone know their intentions. Thus, if it ever happens, you must accept that, however misguided, it was their choice.

Suicide is often chosen as the only way in which depressed people can escape when they are unable to tolerate life as it is any longer. They cannot change it for various reasons, usually involving other people's expectations of them, or expectations they *think* others have of them. Sometimes it is because they believe they can no longer fulfil any useful purpose in life and are a burden to those they love, their friends, or society.

Sometimes suicide may be one final act of hostility towards those who they think will not allow them to change, or one final act of pride.

A failed suicide attempt may be viewed as a very real cry for help. Depressed people have, by that time, usually passed the point at which they can be expected to help themselves. They need help – professional help and the acceptance and support of those close to them. They need to be taken seriously: they cannot just snap out of it – believe me, they would be the first to do just that if they could!

Family Suicide

Most suicidal people believe they've failed in some way. A mother, for example, whose marriage has ended and who has no home or money, may come to believe she's no good as a mother. She can see no future for herself. Tragically, such women are sometimes unable to see any future for their children either. They wish to kill themselves, but cannot bear to leave their beloved children to the mercies of others. Under such circumstances these mothers have taken the lives of their children before their own.

I have come across cases where, having killed her child, a mother has been found and saved from death herself. The unfortunate woman has been treated for her depression and then has to come to terms with life without her child. This remorse must be unbearable.

From time to time there are also reports in the media of fathers in a similar position. A man loses his job, has no money and has to stand by as his family loses its home. His very reason for being, his role as provider, is thwarted.

Men deserted by their wives and left to bring up

children alone have sometimes become desperate. They feel they're failing their children and are failures as men for having been unable to hold on to their wives.

Such men have been known to attempt to kill their families along with themselves.

Accidental Suicide

Many health-care professionals attempt to differentiate between suicide attempts where the person really intended to die, and those which were a dramatic gesture intended to draw attention to an emotional problem, in other words a cry for help.

Most of us have known people who have tried to end a relationship and been told by their partner, 'If you leave me I'll kill myself.' This is a much-used ploy by people who will not face reality and who mistakenly think they can change the way another person feels by coercion.

In most cases, these threats are no more than that. Sometimes the person making the threat will make a gesture such as cutting themselves superficially. Sometimes they will get very drunk and keep saying they want to die. But broken hearts such as these generally mend very quickly. It is often those who complain most that their hearts are irrevocably broken who form new relationships most quickly.

Sadly however, from time to time, an attempt at melodrama backfires. Occasionally, often when drunk, such people take more tablets than they had intended and die by mistake. It is all too often those under 25 to whom this 'accidental' suicide happens.

One such tragic example concerns Natasha. She was only seventeen when she met Stephen. He was thirty. Natasha was flattered that he wanted her of all people. Against her mother's wishes she moved in with him.

Stephen then became more and more possessive, not wanting Natasha to go out with her friends, becoming jealous if she spoke to male classmates at college. Natasha lost touch with her friends, and gave up her ambitions to go to university.

Her mother begged her to return home, pointing out that Stephen was no good for her. Natasha was torn. She loved her mother, but she thought she loved Stephen too and she could not bear to hurt him, even though she hated what was happening to her life because of him.

She repeatedly begged her mother not to make her choose. Her mother, however, couldn't bear what was happening to her once happy, gregarious daughter who was missing out on her youth. She kept on at Natasha whenever she had the chance.

In the end Natasha took an overdose because she couldn't find any alternative. Had her mother just waited and not put on any pressure, things may have resolved themselves eventually. It was thought that Natasha hadn't really wanted to die. She'd simply wanted the emotional pressures upon her to be eased. But she miscalculated.

There are also frequent cases of distraught youngsters who take an overdose on impulse and then change their minds and seek help. Unfortunately, an overdose of some readily available medications, such as paracetamol, is more harmful than is realized and can lead to death from liver failure some days later, long after the person's impulsive desire to die has subsided.

THOSE LEFT BEHIND

Often the loved ones of someone who has committed suicide feel responsible and then angry at the person for not having trusted them to love them enough whatever their problem, and for making them suffer at their death.

Suicide is seen by those left behind as the supreme act of selfishness. But a depressed person cannot conceive how their family and friends will feel at losing them. They cannot bring themselves to care about themselves, so they certainly cannot cope with thinking about the feelings of others! Depressed people have lost all their self-esteem and feel totally worthless – so they can see no reason to believe that anyone else can see anything worthwhile in them or care for them. This state truly is a living hell, totally unimaginable in its desolation to anyone who has not been there.

If someone close to you has committed suicide and you are feeling guilty and angry, remember that you can only move forward when you accept it. We have to accept what we can neither control nor change.

CHAPTER 7

What Help is There?

One of the main problems to overcome with depression is admitting to others that one has it. Many people will not seek help until they find they cannot go on without it. There is a fear that they will be regarded as mentally weak, that it will jeopardize employment prospects, career advancement, life insurance, etc.

It is not surprising that there are close links between alcoholism and depression. People drink to forget, but the depression is still there in the morning, along with the hangover.

In our society, where women are still permitted to show their feelings than men, women with depression seek help more often. Men are afraid of appearing soft. Few people recognize that depression is as much a physical illness as cancer.

It is a strange society where people can be regarded as weak because they have the misfortune to develop depression through no fault of their own. Generally, however, such prejudices arise through fear and lack of knowledge. Many people are very afraid of what they see as going mad. They are afraid of the power of their own minds, they worry about losing control and doing things they would not choose to do. In the minds of much of the public, any psychiatric illness is the first step to madness. However, this makes about as much sense as being afraid each time one catches a cold that it will develop into incurable liver disease.

In the 1970s it was not socially acceptable to be anxious.

Since then, however, stress (the acceptable face of anxiety) has been linked to high-powered jobs, high achievement and conscientiousness. Stress is no longer generally seen as a weakness on the part of the sufferer. It is now viewed as a sign that he or she has worked too hard – it has almost become a status symbol! If one has not had it one cannot have been working hard enough!

The inability to cope with life, whether because of stress, depression or cancer, is still a defect of the whole person. The causes and cures are related not only to either the mind or the body, but to a very complicated interaction between the two. Nobody develops any of these problems through choice, although one may get all or any of them as a result of the way one thinks and behaves in response to what life throws at one. The problem is that society does not recognize this.

There are from time to time articles in magazines in which celebrities admit to having suffered with depression. In time, revelations such as these *will* change the attitudes of the general public, and those who are brave enough to acknowledge their own problems in this way are to be commended.

So what help is available?

HEALTH-CARE PROFESSIONALS

Doctors

Some family doctors are more sympathetic towards mental problems than others. Many prescribe anti-depressants, of which there are many on the market, and it is often a case of finding the right one for each patient. There is a tendency for many cases of depression to be misdiagnosed as anxiety and for tranquillizers to be prescribed when anti-depressants would be more appropriate.

A person with depression may also show signs of anxiety, such as panic attacks. A doctor often does not have the time to analyse the evidence carefully enough to determine the difference. Furthermore, in the early stages of depressive illness, the patient accentuates the anxiety symptoms because these are more unpleasant. Very often he or she will not notice the depression until later.

Psychiatrists

More severe cases of depression are best treated by psychiatrists. They have far greater experience of all the different types of anti-depressant available and will be more likely to find the right one for a particular case. Family doctors will refer patients to a psychiatrist. It does not mean they are going mad. The right anti-depressant will help them recover sooner.

Counsellors

A number of milder depressions are helped by simply talking about the problem. Some doctors now have counsellors attached to their practices. The chance just to talk about their feelings to the counsellor may be enough to make sufferers feel better. The benefits to be gained from talking to someone who does not make judgements about what you are saying are discussed in Chapter 8.

Clinical Psychologists

A doctor may also refer a patient to a clinical psychologist, who will usually use some form of cognitive therapy (cognitive means 'to do with thinking'). This simply means trying to change the way one thinks and views life generally. It is possible that depressed people's usual way of thinking about life and the way they react to it are making them more vulnerable to depression. With help to change their way of thinking, they may be less likely to become depressed again in the future.

There are many different types of such therapy. The important thing is that patients feel that the treatment used is relevant to them. They need to understand their problems in the terms the psychologist describes.

As a clinical psychologist myself I have included in this book some suggestions for ways in which you might be able to help yourself using such methods. These are described in Chapter 9. Obviously, in a general book such as this some of the suggestions will not be as relevant to you as they might be were you having personal treatment. Nevertheless, there may be something that will provide some form of help.

METHODS OF TREATMENT

Anti-depressants

There are people who are reluctant to take any medication at all, especially mood-altering drugs. There is also a fear that such drugs may prove addictive. The public have been frightened by recent reports of tranquillizer addiction and have become wary of anything they perceive as having similar effects.

But anti-depressants are *not* like tranquillizers. They are not generally addictive, nor do they produce instant results as tranquillizers do. An anti-depressant usually has to be taken for two or three weeks before it starts to have an effect. A large proportion of people with depression are helped by the first anti-depressant prescribed for them. Nevertheless, if the first one does not work, or if it produces unacceptable side-effects, tell your doctor. Anti-depressants are not all the same and you may have to find the right one by trial and error.

Electro-Convulsive Therapy (ECT)

ECT is the treatment everyone is afraid of because it has been portrayed on films as a far more barbaric treatment than it actually is. It is not one which should be given lightly, but it does produce dramatic improvement in some very severe cases.

The treatment is administered while the patient is unconscious. Electrodes are placed near the temples and an electric shock delivered to the brain. This causes convulsions, hence the name. A course of treatment usually consists of six such sessions about twice a week.

ECT has proved very effective where anti-depressants have failed. It has never really been understood why it works, although recent findings in relation to changes in the different parts of the brain in depressed people is starting to shed some light on this.

In some parts of the USA there is a vogue for using cranial electrical stimulator (CES) machines. These are small machines which patients can buy on prescription. They deliver a very small electric shock to the surface of the head by means of small electrodes – like a very scaled-down version of ECT . Initial research[12] shows that the use of these machines stimulates the production of certain chemicals and readjusts the balance between them. Many of these chemicals are the same as those contained in anti-depressant drugs, but are made by the body itself. The machines have been found to lift depression in many cases within a couple of weeks. It must be emphasized, however, that no research into the long-term effects of such machines has yet been done so their use cannot be freely recommended.

Light Therapy

This has been found effective in cases of seasonal affective disorder (SAD). Treatment consists of sitting in front of a full-spectrum light for about four hours per day, prefer-ably in the mornings. This is a substitute for bright natural sunlight, the lack of which seems to cause this form of depression. Dramatic improvement can be seen within a week or two.

This is not a treatment that is widely available on the National Health Service in the UK, but it is possible to buy your own special lamp to use at home. However, it is best to be sure that the depression from which you suffer *is* SAD. I have given an address for a supplier of such lamps at the end of the book. It is also possible that if you become a member of the SAD Association (*see* Useful Addresses) they may allow you to hire a light for a trial period to see if it might help you.

FRIENDS AND RELATIONS

Many people can help themselves a great deal simply by being allowed to talk about their feelings to a sympathetic listener. On the other hand, talking to an unsympathetic ear can make one feel a lot worse.

Depression can feel like being lost in a long, dark tunnel. Sometimes just airing one's feelings can show one the chink of light at the end. The listener does not have to offer advice of any kind; sufferers are best left to work out for themselves what is to be done.

The role played by friends and relations is discussed more fully in the next chapter.

CHARITIES AND SELF HELP-GROUPS

Some people who have overcome, or helped close relatives overcome, a particular disorder feel driven to put what they have learnt to use in helping others. Thus many charities and self-help groups have evolved which specialize in various health problems. What they offer ranges from information to regular meetings.

If you feel that you would like to make contact with others who have been through what you are going through – either as a carer or as a sufferer – there is a list of such organizations in the 'Useful Addresses' section.

SPONTANEOUS RECOVERY

Depressions do cure themselves. It is not unusual for someone to be depressed for months and then suddenly, one day, to wake up to find that it has gone. Of course, the same thing happens with headaches, but we all know what treatment is likely to get rid of a headache more quickly, so we take it.

If the depression is only mild, this approach may work. A moderate depression will be more likely to benefit from professional help in order to alleviate the symptoms more quickly. A severe depression definitely needs professional help.

CHAPTER 8

How Family and Friends Can Help

All depressed people need to talk. In order to talk, someone has to listen, but a good listener is a very rare commodity.

People with any type of psychological problem have to work it out for themselves. If solutions are suggested and the sufferer is persuaded to accept them, the result is often only a temporary improvement – if there is any improvement at all. I call this the 'false decision'.

The false decision is the one which a person is talked into. You may recall occasions when this has happened to you. It certainly happened recently to a friend of mine. He was about to buy a new car for the family. He and his wife had carefully weighed all the pros and cons and had concluded that a particular popular estate car was the best buy. It was economical, would carry the loads required, was reliable, etc. But I can still see his face as he told me of their choice – uninspired.

All the logical arguments pointed to that model – all, that is, except that little personal spark of individuality, that little quirk in all of us which means that when we buy something we do not always choose the best buy, the sensible option. 'You really want the Range Rover don't you?' I ventured. His face lit up. The next time I saw him he gave me a lift in it.

Such is the false decision. This is the choice which people either feel obliged to make because it seems the most logical on paper, or the one which others persuade them to make because they do not have an alternative themselves. But a false decision is just that. When it is taken, it is stretched to fit. Once the pressure which was exerted to make it fit in the first place is removed, it springs, like over-stretched elastic, back to its resting position if there is not sufficient shape or motivation within the person it was fitted to keep it there.

This is what happens in bad therapy. A patient will be given an interpretation of his or her symptoms and why they are there. If the patient agrees with this interpretation, and sees the problem in the same terms, then the shape is in place to hold the decision there once the therapist is no longer in evidence, and the patient improves. If, however, the patient cannot quite come to terms with the therapist's interpretation, he or she will simply lapse back once therapy ends.

Because many patients do not have a definite idea of why their problems are there, they need the opportunity to explore the possibilities, to seek out feasible answers for themselves. In short, they need to be able to talk. Patients almost always work out the right answers for themselves if they are given time and occasional prompting with suitable questions.

Thus, a good listener is what depressed people need most: someone who will listen, perhaps comment if asked, but who will not judge or try and persuade them to come to conclusions they do not want or are not ready to reach of their own accord.

This brings us to the next difficulty – personal involvement. In working out what their problem is, sufferers may wish to express feelings and opinions about members of the family or very close friends. It is very difficult for those same friends or relatives to listen impersonally to such disclosures. They will naturally feel hurt or maligned because the sufferer's views and interpretations of their behaviour may not, to their mind, be accurate. But, in order for the sufferer to be helped, his or her opinions must be valued and not simply pushed aside as inaccurate. It is therefore usually best if a sufferer confides in someone who is not personally involved. Thus, in more complicated cases it is generally better to seek professional support, otherwise the problem may escalate to other members of the family.

Those most likely to be helped by other family members or close friends are those who are depressed because of something particular that has happened – the death of someone close, for instance. In cases such as this it usually helps for them to be allowed to talk at length to someone who also knew the person concerned.

They still need someone to listen, however, not someone to tell them to pull themselves together and get on with their life. People who are forced in this way to get over their feelings will simply suppress them. They will go on feeling sad inside, but just not show it. The feelings will still be there and will probably resurface again at some stage, along with resentment towards the person who forced them to smother them earlier – the false decision.

Depressed people need to have their feelings acknowledged. They need to be allowed to feel what they feel for as long as they need to feel it and not to be contradicted or told not to be silly when they dare to express what they truly feel.

Nobody stays depressed if they can help it. It is the most awful, bleak, empty existence imaginable. One feels isolated and unable to care about anything, even though one wishes one could. Telling depressed people to snap out of it only serves to ensure that they hide their true feelings in future.

Those who are depressed are apathetic. They cannot find the energy to tell others exactly how they feel, or what they want, and they do not have the energy to argue. Thus they usually fail to let those closest to them know precisely how they are feeling and what would help them. Often they have not even been able to work it out for themselves. They may only know what they do not want after they have been given it, or realize what they do not want to hear after they have been told it. Rarely do they discover what really helps, because too few of those who care about them really understand.

To someone else, the fact that they feel as they do may appear unjustified, illogical or ungrateful, and they may well agree. But that does not stop them feeling that way and their feelings are all too real. To attempt to deny what they feel is to deny them the right to their feelings. It is to say that your opinion is more valid than theirs. It is this very same failure to accept their feelings which contributes to the depression in the first place.

If people you love are depressed, if you truly want what is best for them, you must allow them to change. You must be prepared to discover that, hidden inside, they may not be the person you always took them to be. You must allow them to become themselves. When they act in ways that are unusual for them, you must not reproach them by saying, 'That's not like you. Why did you do that?' To do that is to deny them their true feelings. It may not be like the 'them' that you have allowed to develop in your mind but it may be the true 'them' that they have always been afraid to reveal until now for fear of ridicule or disapproval.

'I love you' means 'I want you to be happy, I want for you what you want for yourself.' It does not mean 'I want you because *I* need you to perform a particular role in *my* life.'

There are no guilty parties in this. No one is to blame. We have to accept what is and take it from there. As the friend or relative of a depressed person you may need to seek professional advice yourself to help you come to terms with the new person that is sure to emerge as the depression lifts.

So if you are the one that people confide in, then you must do all you can to listen but not judge. Let them talk, perhaps make suggestions, but let them draw their own conclusions. Your role is to help them live through the depression as painlessly as possible.

You have to acknowledge how they feel and the fact that they need to feel like that at this time. You have to allow them to feel what they say they feel. The most frustrating thing for depressed people to hear when they have had the courage to confide in someone is 'You feel depressed? Well how do you think it's making *me* feel?' If you are going to attempt to help you must put your own feelings in the matter aside until much later. You are not the one who's depressed and unable to cope (or if you are then you should be seeking help yourself, not attempting to help others).

Above all, you will need to be patient and seek professional help if you feel unable to cope. It can be emotionally exhausting to sit by while someone you care about suffers, especially when you can do nothing obvious to make them better, and when you can see no obvious improvement.

The elderly and adolescents are especially prone to depression. These are two groups of people whom the rest of us tend to see as being in need of help and guidance, and not capable of being left to make up their own minds about things. Such a patronizing attitude can make vulnerable people, those who have low self-esteem, start to feel out of control and depressed.

Elderly people may become depressed when their lives are restricted by their failing health or lack of money. They may become unable to get out and about as they once did. Lack of money may lead them to feel restricted because they cannot visit their families or give treats to their grandchildren as they would like. As they become older they see no possibility of things ever improving, only becoming worse. Thus they lose hope.

An effort to understand the source of the feelings of elderly people when they become depressed may make it possible to treat the cause. What they need is some hope for the future – as we all do. They need to have the means at their disposal but to have the choice left to them. They need to be able to keep their self-respect and as much control over their lives as possible. It is no surprise that recent research has shown that cantankerous old people who refuse to toe the line live longest. It is the loss of hope and giving up that kills. The elderly may need to be helped to find company if and when they need it, but they do not want to be taken over!

Adolescents become depressed because they often assess their own worth inaccurately. They have no self-esteem so think nobody will find them attractive, give them a job, etc. It is devastating for a teenager not to be allowed to dress and behave as their friends do – it is a very confident youngster who is able to resist peer group pressure.

School bullying is another source of depression. Children may fear the bullying, but fear the reprisals even more if they report it. Most get by by looking forward to leaving school or by truanting. Those who cannot cope become depressed. A child whose behaviour changes at home, who becomes either unusually aggressive or withdrawn, needs careful assessment.

CHAPTER 9

What You Can Do to Help Yourself

It is true that deeply depressed people are too apathetic to do anything to help themselves in the first instance, but then such people would not be reading this! People who are that depressed *must* seek professional help. This chapter is for those who are capable of some self-initiated effort.

One reason why some people succumb to depression whereas others, given the same circumstances, do not, is a difference in the way they think. The way we think is what makes us different from one another. It would be a very boring world indeed if we all thought in the same way. There is no right or wrong way to think about anything. Our thoughts are the one thing we cannot be condemned for – as long as we do not express them aloud. We can think exactly what we please and nobody else need ever know. What freedom!

Unfortunately we are often not aware of the ways in which we think, and we may only come to realize this when we experience psychological problems. Two people can experience identical traumas, yet one person can overcome theirs relatively quickly and emerge unscathed, whereas another may develop PTSD or something similar.

In the same way, it seems that those who suffer from depression do have certain thoughts in common. If they can learn to alter these, then life can seem very different. So what are these thoughts? We will term them 'false beliefs', for reasons that will soon become clear.

FALSE BELIEFS

First, a little experiment. Which of the following two stories do you find the more satisfying?

1 Little Red Hen[13]

You may have read this story as a child. Little Red Hen is out one day and finds a grain of corn. She takes it back to the farmyard and asks the other animals if they will help her plant it. Her so-called friends refuse so Little Red Hen does it herself.

When Little Red Hen asks who will help her water the seed, harvest the corn, take the corn to the mill to be ground into flour and make the flour into bread, the other animals refuse again, so Little Red Hen does it all herself.

Finally she takes the freshly baked bread from the oven and the other animals crowd around, their noses twitching in pleasure. Little Red Hen asks who would help her eat it, and of course this time each animal volunteers.

Then comes Little Red Hen's moment of triumph. She tells them that since none of them helped in the preparations, they are not going to share in the bread. And she eats it all herself!

2 The Prodigal Son

This story is from the Bible. It tells of two brothers, each of whom is one day going to have an inheritance from their father. One of the brothers does not want to wait for his and asks his father if he might have his share early. The father agrees, and the first son goes off on his travels.

The second son is left behind and, consequently has to do his brother's share of the chores as well as his own. Nevertheless, the second son is convinced he is doing the right thing by being dutiful.

The father, however, misses the first son. When, after some years, this son returns home destitute, having spent all his inheritance, the father orders a fatted calf to be killed and a great party to be held to celebrate.

The second son is angry about this. He cannot see why this huge fuss should be made of his brother who shirked his duties and went off and behaved very irresponsibly and then had the nerve to come back penniless and expect to pick up where he had left off. The second son complains to their father. 'Why are you being so nice to him? I've stayed here all the time and done my duty, yet you've never held a party in my honour?'

But their father simply says that he is so pleased to get his son back that all is forgiven.

If you suffer from depression, the chances are that you preferred the story of Little Red Hen, especially the ending. You will have felt that justice was done when the other animals were refused a share of the bread after they had contributed nothing towards it. On the other hand, you feel aggrieved for the second son who did his duty, who did not go in search of the bright lights, even though he may have wanted to. It was not fair that the first son should behave totally irresponsibly and then be forgiven as if nothing had happened.

This experiment illustrates the first of the six false beliefs, which are:

1 **A belief that goodness is rewarded.** If you do your duty, head down, nose to the grindstone, you will get your reward. You will end up better off than those who waste their energies in pleasure when they should be working, etc.

   This is a fallacy. If you expect this to be proved true, you will be disappointed. If you do something solely out of a sense of duty, in the false belief that you *must* be rewarded some time, you will end up disillusioned and bitter, because in this life goodness does not always find its reward. When you do things for others it must be because you want to – for love, for money, in return for something they do for you, because you enjoy it, because you want to, because you have to – but never just because you feel you ought. People who have spent their lives doing things they ought – for no better reason than that – end up depressed when they realize what they have missed.

2 **A belief that you are less deserving than others.** You must put others first or you will be selfish.

This belief is instilled in many people in childhood. This is the problem which the second son in the story had. The trouble is that once you fall into the role of the one others leave to pick up the pieces and carry the burden, you cannot always get out of it. This leads to resentment, often against those who simply allowed you to do what you seemed to want – to run round after them.

3 **A belief that it is bad to get angry.** This relates to the first two. You tend to feel that you do not really have the right to show anger or dissatisfaction. You can always find an excuse for the other person. If you show your real feelings people will not like you or, worse, will be offended.

These first three false beliefs are present even before the depression sets in. They are the typical approach to life of those susceptible to depression. Once such people actually become depressed, even more false beliefs come to the fore.

4 **A belief in 'all or nothing'.** You think things like 'Unless I can do it all, there is no point bothering with any of it', or 'Now I have spoilt my diet today I may as well make the most of it and start again tomorrow.'

5 **A tendency to over-generalize.** You say things like 'I never get it right, nobody cares what I think, nothing good ever happens to me etc.'

6 **An inability to accept things people do for you.** You think things like 'They were only saying that to make

me feel better, it isn't really true', or 'They only want me
to go with them so I can look after their shopping.'

In other words, depressed people are unable to believe
that anyone would want to put themselves out on their
account, or do anything nice for them, unless they had an
ulterior motive. Depressed people are totally unable to
believe that they have any worth at all. They expect nothing
of themselves; if they achieve anything they put it down
to a fluke or a set-up. If people are kind to them or do anything for them, they suspect an ulterior motive.

In view of this, it is easy to see how low self-esteem can
give a person a susceptibility to depression under certain
circumstances. So the route to overcoming depression lies
in developing self-esteem. This cannot be done whilst
people are still very depressed, however, because they
will not accept any such ideas as possible. First they have
to be drawn a little out of their depression so that progress
can be made.

The way out often lies in anger. They suddenly see how
they have been put upon and direct their anger at those
who have put them in that position. This anger and
resentment can be dealt with later – truly confident people
accept responsibility for themselves totally, and if they
have been put upon by others it is because they have
allowed themselves to be.

Thus, in the end, you have to accept the control for
everything *you* do and feel, because you are the only one
who can control your own thoughts. And, as we saw on
page 72, it is our own thoughts that control our destinies,
not what happens to us.

RELIGION

I should say a word here about religion and how some of
the teachings of many religions may conflict with what I
am saying. Many religions teach that it is good to put the
good of others before yourself and to be selfless. I do not

argue with this. It is easier to feel happy and content when you do not want things, especially material things.

The point is that the person has to do these things from a sense of real devotion, not simply because they have been taught that it is what they should do, and been made to feel guilty if they do not. People who behave selflessly because that is the way they feel truly content are the true followers. Such people do not feel pulled in two directions, caught between what they really want to do and be and what they are made to feel they ought to be.

The message here is to be yourself first of all; only then can you be of any use to others. People who are unsure of themselves will be threatened psychologically by the wants and needs of others and will spend all their energies fighting for their own survival.

BREAKING OUT

As I have said, depressed people must become less depressed before they can work on developing true self-esteem. There are ways in which you can begin to change in this way. The aim is to develop an awareness of what you really like, how you really feel, what you really value. In order to do this you have to allow yourself free thought and feeling. Below are some simple exercises to help you do this.

- The most important ingredient in getting better is hope. Without hope, nothing is possible, all avenues are closed. But what is hope?

  It is the possibility of uncertainty, of not knowing exactly what to expect, of allowing yourself to entertain the possibility that things may not turn out precisely as you envisage. Hope is a great adventure. If the future were certain, were already all mapped out, there would be no uncertainty. If everything is certain, what is there to hope for? To hope for something implies that there is a chance it may or may not happen. So do not expect everything to be cut and dried. Allow possibilities to exist. Allow yourself to hope.

- Cut yourself off from the media for a while – do not read newspapers or watch the news on TV. It has been shown that bad news on TV and in the press makes anxious and depressed people even more so. Give yourself a break, avoid it. After all, it is not as if you can help by knowing. Do yourself a favour for a while and switch channels to something light-hearted instead.

  It is probable that our current insistence on conveying bad news from every corner of the world at every opportunity is one of the precipitating factors for stress in our lives. Before mass circulation of such news was possible, people could only worry about their own little corner of the universe. Now we not only have to cope with our own problems, but those of other places too. And it is those people who are psychologically vulnerable, ie already stressed or depressed, who are most affected by it. A break from time to time is good for you. If you have ever been abroad, you will know how wonderful it is to be totally unaware of the rest of the world's disasters. Indulge yourself and switch off more often.

- Indulge in right brain activity. Allow yourself to become lost in something creative. It is amazing how few people ever do anything creative. We are always analysing, working out things in our heads, putting things in order, running to schedule – all things which use the left side of the brain. The right side, the creative, intuitive, feeling side, needs exercise too.

  Creative activity can be anything, such as cooking – providing you enjoy it, and are creating and experimenting – sewing, knitting, painting, decorating, gardening, playing a musical instrument, dancing, sailing, horse-riding, writing stories, poems or letters. The important thing is that you try not to think, just to feel, simply allowing your body to indulge in the activity without judging your performance. It is the doing that is important – not how well you do it.

- Take some physical exercise. Regular physical activity of any kind you find enjoyable is known to be beneficial to the person as a whole. We were, after all, designed originally to be physically active.

  If you are not used to doing anything like this, begin with taking a short walk each day, and enjoying it – smell the air, listen to the different sounds, notice colours. You may have to make yourself do all these things to begin with, but after a while you will become more appreciative of everything around you.

- Keep a diary of what you have achieved each day. There must be no negative thoughts or aspects in it. Put down new sights and smells, new experiences of any kind. Note down everything that you have done during the day, no matter how insignificant – what you have read that has been interesting and why, what you have thought and felt that was interesting, and why. But there must be no mention of feeling bad!

- Make a list of things you must do each day and tick them off as you go – this gives you a sense of achievement. If you think of something pleasant and self-indulgent that you would rather do than one of your chores, then do it and enjoy it – and then write about it.

- Care for something or someone that needs you. For instance, plant something in the garden, and tend it and watch it grow, look after someone's pet for them, spend some time helping out because you *want* to rather than because you have to or feel you should.

- Find someone to listen. You need to talk in order to work out for yourself what it is you really want. You need a confidant to bounce ideas off – someone who will listen but not judge. It needs to be someone who is not involved in the causes of your depression – perhaps a good friend who can be trusted not to gossip. If you know of no one, find a counsellor.

- Laugh. Even when you just make laughing expressions, your body produces chemicals that make you feel happier. Watch films or TV programmes that you enjoy. Listen to jokes you enjoy.

- 'Turn the dark into light'. List all the negative incidents in your life that come to mind, such as when you failed an examination, when you had a bad fall, any incident which gives you bad memories.

Now take one incident from the list and rewrite it in neutral terms – just write what happened, without judgements or feelings, just a description of the incident itself as it might have been seen by an observer who did not know any of the background, as if you were watching it happen as a passer-by.

For instance, if the incident was falling off a pony, you might write:

A little girl in a blue dress was helped onto the pony by the man who owned them. The pony was led along the beach. Suddenly a large beach ball bounced right in front of the pony's nose and made it jump. The little girl fell off and ended up on the sand with her skirt over her head.

Now forget any anger or embarrassment the incident caused and rewrite it, ignoring anything that feels bad and concentrating only on the good aspects of the incident – those aspects which you have almost forgotten because your mind has been focusing on the negative ones. For example:

I remember the pony's nose, soft as velvet. I remember feeling happy as I swayed across the sand on its back, pretending I was a film star. Then, when I fell off, the sand was dry and soft and I sank into it.

Next read this last version each day and picture the scene as vividly as you can as you do so. Try and recall all the good bits, the smell of the sea, the happy mood, how the sunshine felt on your bare arms, etc. If you are able to do a relaxation exercise it will be more powerful if you do this visualization when you are relaxed. Or you could lie back in a warm bath, close your eyes, let go and do it there.

Repeat the same incident each day until you feel that you have done it enough and the positive side is appearing easily. Then move on to the next incident and repeat the exercise with that, by rewriting it in a neutral and a positive way and visualizing the positive.

For those negative aspects of your life which are present each day, ask yourself if you have to have them. If not, give them up. If you have to put up with them – you may, for instance, have a job you find boring but which you cannot afford to lose – see it as a challenge to find some positive elements to concentrate on. There is nothing to be gained by having to do something you dislike whilst constantly telling yourself how much you hate it and wish you were not doing it. This is resistance and too much of it can lead to anxiety and depression. Practise accepting what you must do and putting your energy into focusing on something pleasant instead.

For example, if you hate having to produce tables of results, see if you can devise a way of doing it as efficiently and quickly as possible. This will at least present you with a more interesting mental challenge and will give you something positive at the end – your own performance. If you have to do repetitive tasks that do not require great concentration – making beds in a hotel, for instance – you could imagine you are cleaning the room of someone famous and really see if you can pretend they are there!

Use the power of your own imagination to help you through the duller parts of life.

- Be patient. Unless you know why you are depressed and can begin to make plans to do something about it, take one day at a time. Allow yourself to be content with what you do as you do it. Spend a part of each day pretending to be happy. By this I mean be like an actor and pretend you are playing the role of someone happy. Try and let yourself really *be* that character.

This may sound a silly idea, but it works. What we *pretend* to be, we end up actually being. It has been found that it is not necessarily having too many negative things in our lives that gets us down, but not having enough positive ones.

So enjoy each moment as best you can. Focus your thoughts on the little positive things. Listen to your favourite music, have bubbles in your bath, eat something indulgent. There is nothing wrong with pleasure as long as you do not cause anyone pain as a result.

Do not let your mind race forward in time to 'what if' and do not dwell on what is past and on 'if only'.

One thing about depression is that it seems eventually to lift of its own accord even if you do nothing at all. If you do something it lifts all the sooner.

It may be difficult to overcome by yourself, so do not be afraid to seek professional help if you need it. You must also be aware that, as you get better and find your self-esteem, you may find that certain of your loved ones may become less welcoming to the changes in you. But that is their problem.

CHAPTER 10

Relationships and Depression

A good relationship, in which those involved accept one another as they are and are supportive when required, can help prevent depression. A bad relationship, on the other hand, can cause it.

People whose hopes, aspirations and expectations are constantly unfulfilled are greatly at risk. And relationships in which one person is far more dominant than the other, and leads their partner to believe he or she must behave in a certain way, can be very damaging. The non-dominant partner often wants the approval of the other, tries to live up to the dominant one's expectations and feels inadequate if he or she fails.

Here are examples of various sorts of relationships which were damaging in this respect.

Shona was the daughter of an ambassador from an African country. She came to the UK to study law. At home she had been her father's favourite and he had always expected great achievements from her. In Britain, however, Shona found the different culture, the climate, and a certain amount of racial prejudice difficult to cope with. She felt low. Her studies suffered because she slowly lost the ability to motivate herself sufficiently. One day she received a final demand from the electricity company saying she had not paid her bill and the supply would be cut off.

Shona had overlooked the bill. She had also run out of money. She felt so guilty and such a failure that she could not approach her father for money, even though he would have given it. It was just too much and she tried to kill herself.

What had happened in Shona's case was that she had, little by little, allowed her self-esteem to ebb away. Finally, without it, she felt worthless.

In a perfect relationship each person starts as he or she means to go on, truthfully. In the vast majority of relationships, we start with untruths and carry on like that. If you are keen on someone, you may hide those aspects of yourself which you think might put him or her off – you are on your best behaviour. However the other person tends to assume that this is the real you, and expects the behaviour to continue. When it does not – having been something of an false decision in the first place and a real effort to keep up for too long – the other person is disenchanted and claims that you have changed. In reality you have simply become the real you.

In many relationships, the real you is accepted and life goes on albeit a little less magically than before. In some, however, one person is afraid to reveal their true self, or the other person refuses to accept it, and life becomes a lie. This is the breeding ground for disaster. The elastic is in place around a false shape and it becomes more and more of an effort to keep it there.

There are two extreme types of people – givers and takers. It seems that we become like this in childhood when we either get used to having our way and others giving in to us, or we get used to always being the one who has to back down, who has to lend their toys even when we do not want to. Takers then grow up to say what they really feel and expect others to react accordingly. They never doubt that others will do as they expect. If they do not, takers make a fuss until they get their way.

Many relationships have a giver and a taker. The taker is the one whose choices are adopted when there is disagreement. The taker is the one the rest of the family try not to upset.

However, takers are unaware of this. They assume that everyone thinks like them. They believe that anyone who disagrees will say so. They have no concept of giving in for a quiet life.

Therefore, when one day the giver in the relationship decides that he or she cannot go on any more cycling holidays, for example, and says in a fit of rage that he or she has always hated them, the taker is totally bewildered and says, 'But you've never said!' Takers simply cannot conceive how people could put up with not getting their own way.

Takers will protest and claim that they do give – they give presents for example. This is true, but the actual act of giving is not what makes one a giver or taker. When takers buy presents they buy what they want the other person to have, not necessarily what that person most wants. In many ways takers are control freaks – people who want to control not only their own needs and feelings, but also those of the people important to them, the people they claim to love.

Givers, on the other hand, have learnt from childhood not to make a fuss, to give in for a quiet life. Of the two it is givers who tend to end up with depression. They reach a stage where they glimpse what life could be like if they did what they wanted for a change. But they cannot make the change because nobody expects them to behave like that, nobody takes them seriously.

A giver can become something of a chameleon – changing constantly so as to fit in with the needs of others. Because of their role in society, many married women who have been bringing up children tend to fall into this category. They deny their own wishes so as to put those of their children first.

This inevitably restricts their personal freedom, so they deny even more of their desires. Their husbands then tend to assume that they have none. They get so accustomed to being whatever others expect them to be that they lose sight of who they really are. One day they realize that they do not seem to exist in their own right. They feel helpless, hopeless and non-existent. They develop depression.

Elizabeth was the elder of two sisters. She was three years old when her sister, Christine, was born and was wildly jealous. She resented having to share her parents, her pram and her bedroom with this noisy baby. When she was five she started school. Christine stayed at home alone with their mother, and Elizabeth resented this. She resented even more the fact that, while she was at school, Christine was allowed to play with Elizabeth's toys. Very often the first thing Elizabeth did on arriving home from school each day was to march up to her younger sister, hit her and destroy whatever she was playing with.

Elizabeth repeatedly begged her mother not to allow Christine to play with her toys, but their mother simply crooned, 'Don't be selfish, Elizabeth, she isn't hurting them.'

As the sisters grew older they got on better and played together. But if ever there was a difference of opinion between them, it was always Christine who yelled the loudest, and who got her own way. Elizabeth said later that, looking back, she developed the belief that she did not really matter and had no right to put her needs before those of others. She almost came to expect that whatever she valued would be borrowed or taken by others.

Thus, later in life, she fell all too easily into the domestic role, putting the needs of her family first, unable even to recognize what her own needs might be. Nobody had ever taken her beliefs or desires seriously, so she had stopped voicing them, and had even stopped thinking about them.

She had developed the ability to be whatever others expected of her. If she went to dinner with her husband and his friends, she dutifully made small talk. If she went to an open day at the children's school, she discussed their progress. When the family went on holiday, she chose places where her husband and children could enjoy themselves.

Elizabeth had become a chameleon. She adapted her beliefs and her behaviour and to her surroundings so as to fit in harmoniously. But it was not her.

One day, unforseen circumstances led her to spend time with a group of total strangers who knew nothing about her at all. To them she was neither her children's mother nor her husband's wife. She suddenly tasted the freedom of being able to be exactly who she wanted to be, to be who she really was. She glimpsed the untainted sky and there could be no going back.

We all think we know what love is, but few of us truly practise it. True love allows people to be who they really are and accepts them for that. True love does not try to change people into what we would prefer them to be. True love accepts them for what they are.

You cannot force someone to love you, no matter how much you may want to. Love has to be freely given, for no reward.

Love is like befriending a wild animal. Suppose one day a deer came into your garden and nibbled your shrubs. Suppose you liked its being there and wanted it to stay. What would you do? You could trap it, lock it in and prevent it from leaving. The deer would be forced to stay in your garden, but it would not be happy. It would lose its natural tendencies and would probably become listless and uninterested.

It might eat the food you gave it, it might eventually get used to you and not show fear. But if you ever left the garden gate open accidentally, it would probably run away. Because no matter how kind you had been, it would still prefer to take its own chances in the wild and make its own choices, rather than live its life in captivity. Alternatively, it would become so dependent on you for its existence that it would lose its true wild nature and its will to live freely. It would stay with you as a spiritless dependant.

If, however, when the deer first wandered into your garden, you made no attempt to trap it, but simply offered it food, it might eat. It might wander away and never return. It might, however, return to see if it could have more food. It might keep returning of its own free will.

The deer that has freedom to leave or return is like love. Love has to be given freely, with no expectation of reward. True love means wanting for people what they want for themselves. Loving is not keeping people with you because they are too afraid to leave. Loving is not changing people to the way you want them to be. Loving is allowing them to be what they want to be and accepting them as such. To truly love another person is the most difficult thing in the world.

The relevance here is that many depressed people are kept emotionally imprisoned because they cannot bear to hurt those they love. So they get caught in an impossible situation of either denying themselves or hurting those they love. They choose the former.

But this self-denial can become too much and cause deep depression. This was the case with Elizabeth who, having realized that she wanted to break out of her prison, was unable to do so without hurting those she loved, those who claimed to love her, but who saw her as a very different person from the one she really was inside.

Very often depressed people are told by their loved ones, 'I only want what's best for you, stand up for yourself.' The trouble is that what they really mean is 'Stand up for yourself with other people but not with me.' Close relatives can be very resistant to changes in those they have taken for granted.

Catriona was a confident young ballet dancer before her marriage to Alex, a school teacher. When her daughter was born she began teaching ballet. She continued to do this even after her son was born a couple of years later.

Over the years, however, Alex slowly wore her down. He criticized her in small ways – why had they run out of marmalade, why were his shirts not starched, why did she not cook an Indian meal for a change? He was also highly critical of their daughter in that nothing she ever did was praised. Instead he asked why she had not done a tiny bit better and come top of the class instead of third.

When they went on holiday Catriona found it a constant

drain on her because Alex seemed to expect her to know the answers to everything and to have prepared for every eventuality. She invariably returned totally shattered from the constant stress of being criticized all day every day. She was also worried about the effect it was having on their daughter, who was becoming anxious and withdrawn.

Eventually Catriona became depressed. She told Alex what she had really felt all those years, and he said he would change. But nothing happened. She suggested they sought marriage counselling but Alex repeatedly made excuses not to keep the appointments. One day she took the children and moved out.

At this Alex became distraught and begged her to come back, saying he would change. Catriona refused. Then the two children began to ask for their father – he had apparently been pressurizing them when he spent time with them, saying how sad he was and how much he missed them.

In the end Catriona succumbed and went back, only to find that nothing had changed at all. By this time she was in a situation she could see no way out of. She wanted to leave Alex but the children made her feel guilty. She could not leave the children with him because of the effect on them of his endless criticism.

Since Alex never kept counselling appointments, Catriona went herself. Over some months she developed self-esteem. When she stood up to Alex and his criticisms he would say, 'That's not like you!'

This is a giveaway. When anyone says this to you, what they mean is, 'I don't expect you to behave like that, I want you to behave as I expect.' Such a comment is often a good sign that you are being a real person, not simply the puppet they have been accustomed to manipulating for their own ends.

The truth is that, generally speaking, however much you put yourself out for others, especially if you do it in the expectation of being liked in return, rather than because you *want* to do it, the less they think of you and the more they put upon you. You will end up feeling used and depressed. If you avoid rows and opt instead for the quiet life, you will end up as someone else's prop, not expected to have desires and needs of your own – which is fine, as long as you have none!

I am not advocating total selfishness, simply that the givers of this world should become more conscious of what they give, how often they give in, and why. It is perfectly all right to *choose* to give in. It is when you do it automatically, against your own interests, because you are afraid not to, that it becomes ominous.

In the end Catriona took the children and left Alex for good.

Barbara, a lecturer, found that her lawyer husband, John, became kinder and more attentive when she suffered a severe bout of depression. Hating herself for being pathetic and dependent, she expected him to be cross with her too. It turned out that, in spite of the fact that he always maintained that he was in favour of independent career women, he did not really believe it.

His own parents had a traditional middle-class marriage where his mother stayed at home and cooked cakes and casseroles while his father followed his career. His father controlled the finances and gave his mother housekeeping money and a dress allowance – to be spent on making herself attractive for him.

Like Catriona's, Barbara's depression was traced to years of being made to feel guilty at not being a 'proper' wife and mother. She had raised two children whilst continuing to work – part time whilst they were young. John had never done any household chores or taken any responsibility for child care. His career had had to come first, and he had worked long hours.

It was significant that, once Barbara became better, lost her guilt complex and began to challenge John's snide disapproval, he became less pleasant. Eventually he left her for a younger woman who doted on him whom, he thought, he could mould into his very own Stepford Wife.

It is not only women who suffer in this way, however. Such difficulties also affect men, as was mentioned in Chapter 3. Men often become confused. They live according to how they were taught and then find their efforts are resented by women. One of the main reasons for this is many of today's men were taught how to treat women by their fathers, or copied their fathers' examples. The problem is that society has changed rapidly in this respect since the 1960s. Today's women do not want to be treated as their mothers were. In many cases they regard it as insulting, and resist fiercely.

This leaves large numbers of men totally perplexed as to how to behave in what, to them, is one of the most important areas of their lives, their ability to attract and keep a mate. At a very basic level, the male of virtually every species has procreation as his main goal. It is the reason for his existence. In females, however, in many species once pregnancy is achieved, the male becomes insignificant and is disregarded. The female is then more concerned with safeguarding her offspring.

The lives of human beings are far more complex than this. Nevertheless, our most primitive instincts are still there and will take over to ensure the survival of the species whenever our higher levels of thinking or behaviour break down.

When we become unsure of ourselves, we are anxious about situations which we can normally persuade ourselves to face. We worry about change and want to cling to old patterns and routines. When men feel they are failing in their personal relationships and in their ability to attract and keep a female companion, they tend to become depressed and anxious because their basic instincts are being thwarted.

There is often a strange contradiction I find when discussing sexual fidelity with men. Many men claim that they would secretly like to have sex with an attractive stranger, purely without emotional involvement, as a one-night stand. Even men in stable, one-to-one relationships admit this desire even though they would probably never submit to it. When asked, however, why their wife or partner should not do the same, they come out with comments such as, 'Why would she want someone else? Aren't I good enough?'

Robert had recently separated from his wife of 15 years. They had no children and realized they no longer had the same goals in life, so concluded they might as well go their separate ways.

Robert then claimed he only wanted casual relationships with no ties. He proceeded to become involved with two different women in succession, both of whom eventually terminated their relationship with him because he was too possessive and controlling.

His second girlfriend, Julia, was a single mother. She lived with her mother and worked full-time to support herself and her daughter. She rarely went out in the evenings, preferring to stay at home and relax. At weekends she wanted to spend time with her child.

Robert worried about her lack of social life and tried to make her go out more. He also wanted to give both her and her daughter a good time at weekends. He was very upset when Julia resisted his plans.

I tried to explain to Robert that Julia had the right to live her own life as she saw fit and that she did not necessarily share his views of what constituted a good time. He countered this with comments such as, 'I only wanted to look after her and give her a good time!'

This attitude was deeply entrenched in the way he saw his parents' marriage, and how he saw the traditional role of the man – to look after his woman and give her a good time. But Julia was a 'new woman' and preferred to look after herself.

Robert began to grow depressed because, as far as he knew, he was behaving exactly as he had been brought up, but this was leading to failure in his relationships. To overcome this he has to undergo a huge change in his attitude towards women and their role in society if he is to form any kind of relationship with the type of woman he seems to prefer. A relationship with a more traditional type of woman might be fine, but Robert prefers strong, independent women!

Generally, then, it would seem that relationship difficulties of various kinds contribute to the development of a great many depressive illnesses. We all need to be far more aware of what we expect of one another and of what we ought to expect. A healthy relationship is supportive but allows each partner to be the person they want to be and accepts them as such.

CHAPTER 11

Is Depression Avoidable?

Until we can find out for certain what chemical changes occur when someone becomes depressed, and find out what triggers them, will not even begin to be able to discover whether one can avoid depression. As with a tendency towards anxiety, it does appear that some people are more inclined to become depressed than others. We cannot say, however, that anyone has actually avoided depression until we are able to expose people to its cause and observe their minds and bodies resisting it as a result of some kind of preventive action. Nevertheless, if we consider what depressed people regard as the causes of their illnesses, it may offer some guidance as to possible preventative measures.

THINKING

We already know that two people can experience identical events and yet one may become depressed as a result whereas the other does not. The only difference between them is the way in which they think about what has happened and how it affects them.

The way we think affects the way our body behaves and this in turn influences the way we feel. The best example is the case of fear. Fear is triggered by a thought. When we come across something we are afraid of, we think things such as, 'Oh, I don't like this! What if I get hurt?' This fear message is acted on by the brain which makes the heart beat faster, drains blood from the surface of the skin to feed more essential muscles and organs, and generally prepares us to escape. We therefore develop bodily symptoms as a direct result of what we think. In the same way, certain ways of thinking can probably make someone feel depressed. The change is, however, slower and less dramatic than is the case with fear.

Many of us fail to live up to our own aspirations, let alone those that others have for us. If we constantly keep a mental tally of our 'failures' in this respect, then we are storing the ammunition for depression.

What we have to learn is *acceptance*. We have to accept ourselves just as we are. We can do our best to improve ourselves, but we should not set too much store by it. There is nothing wrong with daring to have a go at something at which one may not succeed – as long as one puts it down to experience if one fails and moves on. The past is for learning from, then letting go. All too often we try to carry all our burdens with us into the present.

There is a story about two monks who were walking one day. They came to a stream, at the edge of which was a very beautiful woman wearing very short shorts and a low-cut T-shirt. The woman was crying because the stream was flowing too fast and she was afraid to cross it. One of the monks invited her to jump onto his back and carried her across. When they reached the other side the two monks bade the woman goodbye and went on their way. Several miles and some hours later the second monk turned to his gallant companion. 'I'm sure you committed several sins back there, brother,' he said.

The first monk smiled. 'I left the woman behind long ago on the riverbank,' he said. 'It's a pity you didn't do the same.'

The moral of this tale is that no matter what has happened, be it good or bad, it is within the power of each of us to let go of that which is of no further pleasure or benefit to us. Too few of us actually live in the present, enjoying each moment as it is upon us. All too often our minds are either in the future, worrying about what might be or what has to come next, or stuck in the past in guilt or regret over something that cannot possibly be changed. None of us has the power to change anything that has already happened. What each of us does have, however, is the power to change the way we think about it or remember it.

New research suggests that what we need to allow to develop is our creative, imaginative side. Remember the last time you read a novel – how your mind constantly provided pictures of what was happening as you read? It may turn out that the present obsession with video presentations of everything is going to prove detrimental in the long term because it no longer allows us to use this totally individual and creative ability known as visualization.

Visualization has already been shown to be a powerful tool in helping people overcome various illnesses. It is now thought that our ability to picture in our minds our body's defences getting up and overcoming tumours, for example, can trigger them to take over and do the job themselves. Hence, our minds influence our bodies!

An experiment I read about recently involved a group of people who were in hospital with bleeding ulcers. They were given injections of what they were told was a 'new experimental drug' which might or might not help them. What they actually received was sterile water. Seventy per cent of the group believed they had received a cure and improved remarkably. The 'cure' was still working a year later.

Those who are most open-minded and prepared to use their imaginations, and to accept possibilities for which they see no valid scientific reason, are the most successful at 'jump-starting' the body's own ability to heal itself. Those who are not prepared to accept these possibilities until everything has been scientifically proven beyond doubt, are not very effective at summoning 'miracle' cures for themselves.

It has been found that we remember incidents according
the way we felt at the time. This is called state-depend
memory, and it means we do not remember the past
neutral terms, seeing both sides of any situation. Rath
we remember it according to whether it felt good or b
and the emotional state we were in. We are less able
recall those incidents which were not steeped in any k
of strong emotion at the time. Similarly, once an inci
has been associated with a particular feeling, we tend to
the same way about similar incidents. Thus, if you fel
when you went to Aunt Mary's for lunch, the chan
you may tend to feel queasy when you go the nex
you fall in love on holiday in Rhodes, you will al
a soft spot for the place, unless you go back the
a bad time, in which case your memories are de

The rule is therefore to try and allow yo
something positive in everything, mentally la
and different situations as 'exciting' rather th
ing'. This is what those who seem to be able
life and everything it throws at them are able
find something positive in even the worst tha
then you have cracked it!

ACCEPTANCE

We only have the power to control our own thoughts a
actions. No matter how much we try and control othe
we cannot. If we try to control others, they will keep aw
or will give in to the requests but secretly resent us. I ha
already touched on this subject in Chapter 8. We m
accept other people just as they are; it is up to them
change themselves if they want to. Nobody has the right
control another. The only possible exception to this i
parent's right to hold control of a child in trust until t
child is able to take over.

LFISH OR SELF-CONFIDENT?

fish people are those who put themselves first and who
ect other people to give up their own desires in favour
theirs. To be selfish is also to be self-obsessed, to be
cerned with how everything affects one all the time.

n contrast, self-confident people know who they are.
y know that nobody can change them and the way
y are unless they choose to let them. This is something
en have to spell out to patients seeking help. Some
le expect a therapist to be able to wave a magic wand
make their troubles disappear. Then they blame the
ist when the magic does not work. So I always
oint of explaining that whilst I can offer guidance
uragement, I cannot actually change people's
king – they have to be prepared to allow that
or themselves.

eakness to give in to the demands of others, as
are able to choose to do so. The person who is
is the strongest. You only have to make a
hat is really important to you.

an oak tree beside a river. At its foot grew a
lay the oak tree would chastise the reed for
y bending this way and that to the will of the
Look at me, little reed,' the oak would say. 'See
I yield to no one, for I am an oak and I am strong.'
reed said nothing; there was no point.

ne night a terrible storm came. The wind blew
cely, far more strongly than usual. In the morning the
tree was broken in two, but the little reed still stood at
oot, swaying in the sunshine.[14]

LANCE THEORY

ether it is treated or not, depression seems to disap-
r quite suddenly. It may take weeks or over a year, but
appens. It may come back if the conditions which

caused it are repeated, but it seems that the body adjusts itself to the imbalance in the system and rights itself – until the next time.

It seems that our bodies never tolerate extremes of emotion for very long. Think of the ecstasy of a new love – the kind where you feel as if you are floating on air, you cannot concentrate, cannot eat, where you are on a high. This never lasts either. We create endorphins – neurochemicals that make us feel wonderful – but, as with every other new sensation, after a while we overload and our cells stop responding.

The 'high' of being in love is created within us, by our own thoughts about the person concerned, and our own need to feel such emotion at that time. The fact that it seems to happen so much more often during our teens appears to suggest that it could be triggered by hormonal changes. Nevertheless there is still a large degree of our own thinking needed to make it actually happen. It is not unreasonable, then, to assume that depression is triggered by similar bodily changes combined with our thoughts, but what triggers the bodily changes is still uncertain.

We are responsible for the way we are, no one else. We cannot ultimately blame anyone else for our problems; the remedy rests with us alone. It is not especially important what happened to us in the past, what our parents did or did not do. What *is* important is the way we think about what happened. We cannot change the past but we can change the way we remember it. Often the crux of coping with depression and getting through it is to change our way of thinking.

To avoid depression take responsibility for your own life. Learn from the past and let go of it. Accept what you cannot change and trust yourself.

Notes

1 Sue Breton, *Don't Panic*, Optima, 1986
2 G W Brown and T Harris, *Social Origins of Depression*, Cambridge University Press, Cambridge, 1978
3 J Price, 'Neurotic and Endogenous Depression: A Phylogenic View,' *British Journal of Psychiatry*, Vol 114, 1968
4 Brown and Harris, *Social Origins of Depression*
5 M Hutchinson, *Mega Brain Power*, Hyperion, New York, 1994
6 Sack et al, 'Biological Rhythms in Psychiatry', in Metzer (ed), *Psychotherapy: The Third Generation of Progress*, Raven Press, New York, 1987
7 D Healy and J M G Williams, 'Dysrhythmia, Dysphoria and Depression. The Interaction of Learned Helplessness and Circadian Dysrhythmia in the Pathogenesis of Depression,' *Psychological Bulletin*, Vol 103, 1988
8 R J Davidson et al, 'Approach-Withdrawal and Cerebral Asymmetry: Emotional Expression and Brain Physiology,' *Journal of Personality and Social Psychology*, Vol 58, 1990
9 C McCullough, *The Thornbirds*, Macdonald and James, London, 1977
10 D Rowe, *Depression: The Way Out of Your Prison*, Routledge and Kegan Paul, London, 1983
11 E M Forster, *Collected Short Stories*, Penguin, 1947
12 C N Shealy et al, 'Depression – A Diagnostic Neurochemical Profile and Therapy with Cranial Electrical Stimulation (CES),' *Journal of Neurological and Orthopedic Medicine and Surgery*, Vol 10, 1989
13 *The Little Red Hen*, Ladybird Books, Loughborough, 1983
14 Adapted from La Fontaine, *Fables: Le Chêne et Le Roseau*, Garnier, Flammarion, Paris, 1966

Glossary

Acceptance Taking the way things are as your starting point rather than pretending they are as you might wish them to be.

Accidental Suicide When someone makes it look as if they are attempting suicide in order to get people to listen to them or pay attention to their needs, but they miscalculate and die.

Adjustment Disorder Psychological difficulty in adapting to a different way of life, causing anxiety and/or depressive symptoms.

Affective Disorder When someone experiences moods that are not appropriate to his or her circumstances, or which are inappropriately intense.

Anti-Depressants Drugs whose main purpose is to remove symptoms of depression.

Biochemicals Natural chemical substances created by the body.

Bipolar Depression A form of depressive illness where the person experiences periods of both abnormally high and abnormally low moods.

CFS Chronic Fatigue Syndrome (also thought to be similar to, or the same as, Myalgic Encephalomyelitis or ME) often occurs after a viral infection. The sufferer becomes very tired and listless for no real reason. May last from months to years.

Circadian Rhythm A biological pattern based on a daily cycle of about 24 hours, eg sleeping and eating.

Clinical Depression A 'low' mood which is deeper than is normal and/or which continues for an abnormally long time.

Depressive Phase Periods of 'low' mood experienced by someone who has a bipolar disorder.

ECT Electro-Convulsive Therapy is the administration of a controlled electric shock to the brain, usually to lift a depression.

Empowerment Giving real power to the decisions made by people, usually in a work environment, ie people are not encouraged to make decisions only to have them over-ruled by someone 'higher up.'

Endogenous Depression An old description of a depression due to and maintained by chemical changes from within the body and thus not able to be changed by 'thinking your way out of them.'

Endorphins The chemicals produced by the body which give a 'high' feeling. These are so-called because they are a form of 'endogenous morphine' ie a drug produced within the body itself which gives the person a 'high' similar to that produced by taking morphine.

Environmental Influences Influences of other people or lifestyle or our way of living. Any influences which do not come from within ourselves.

Euphoria A feeling of being on a 'high'. This is a common symptom of the manic phase of a bipolar depression.

False Belief Beliefs held by depressed people, usually about themselves, which they believe and act on but which have absolutely no justification. Beliefs such as, 'Everything I do is wrong.'

False Decision When a person is 'talked into' a particular decision against their real wishes.

Family Suicide When a parent with a depressive illness not only sees no future for him or herself but can see none for the children either, so takes the lives of the children too.

Genetic Influences Those tendencies we are born with because they are inherited in our genes.

Helplessness When you feel unable to influence what is happening in your own life, even though you feel you ought to be able to.

Hopelessness When you feel there is no way out of your predicament.

Hormones Chemicals released into the bloodstream by a particular gland or tissue that has a specific effect on tissues elsewhere, eg the effect of oestrogen on reproductive system.

Immune System A collection of cells and proteins that work to protect the body from potentially harmful infectious micro-organisms.

Insomnia The inability to follow what is regarded as a normal sleep pattern.

Love Accepting someone you care deeply for as they are and allowing them to live as they wish.

Mania The 'high' phase of a bipolar depression.

Manic Describes a person in the 'high' phase of a bipolar depression. Someone who is abnormally high spirited and happy when conditions do not really warrant it.

Manic Depressive Psychosis A bipolar depression in which the sufferer has phases of both 'downs' and 'ups' ie of both high and low mood.

Masked Depression A depression which is not immediately obvious because the main symptoms are of something else, eg anxiety.

Mild Depression The first stage of depressive illness where only a few symptoms are noticed. This stage may be overcome with self-help measures.

Moderate Depression The second stage of depressive illness. The symptoms, such as sleep problems and negative thoughts, are more intrusive. The sufferer may need help.

Mood Disorder Any abnormal mood, be it abnormal happiness or sadness, when nothing has happened to justify it.

Neurotransmitter A chemical released from nerve endings that transmits impulses from one nerve cell to another or to a muscle.

Personality State The mood you are in. This may change depending upon circumstances, and is always a passing thing.

Personality Trait A fairly permanent aspect of your personality which colours the way you interpret what goes on around you eg whether you are a pessimist or an optimist.

PTSD Post Traumatic Stress Disorder follows when the sufferer experiences something profoundly distressing, such as a major disaster. Some weeks or months afterwards they become anxious and/or depressed.

Reactive Depression An old definition for a depressive disorder that was thought to be due to unfortunate circumstances. For instance, being depressed due to redundancy.

Recurrent Disorder A disorder which gets better but which then comes back again at various intervals.

REM Rapid Eye Movement denotes a particular period of the normal sleep cycle during which we dream. People who are systematically prevented from having this stage become very disturbed.

SAD　Seasonal Affective Disorder is the depression caused by insufficient sunlight.

Severe Depression　The third stage of depressive disorder when the sufferer is no longer really able to help him or herself. Professional help should be sought.

State-Dependent Memory　Memories which occur during a particular state or mood and which are then associated with that mood.

Suicide　The act of taking one's own life.

Tranquillizers　Drugs whose primary aim is to calm down a person.

Unipolar Depression　A depression which only features lowered mood in varying degrees.

Further Reading

Sue Breton, *Why Worry*, Element, 1994
This book describes positive thinking techniques in greater detail.

Sally Burningham, *Young People Under Stress: A Parent's Guide*, Virago, 1994
Philip J Barker, *A Self-Help Guide to Managing Depression*, Chapman & Hall, 1993
Professor Robert Priest, *Anxiety and Depression*, Optima, 1992
Dr Richard Gillett, *Overcoming Depression*, Dorling Kindersley, 1994
Andrew Canale, *Beyond Depression*, Element, 1992
Bloomfield and McWilliams, *How to Heal Depression*, Thorsons, 1995
Dorothy Rowe, *Breaking the Bonds*, HarperCollins, 1991
David Kinchin, *Post Traumatic Stress Disorder*, Thorsons, 1994

Also, to help safeguard future good health:
More Positive Thinking by Vera Peiffer, Element, 1995

And for those confused by relationship difficulties:
Positively Single by Vera Peiffer, Element, 1995

Supplier of lamps for light therapy:
Lifetools
Freepost SKI852
Macclesfield
Cheshire SK10 2YE, UK
Tel. 01625 502602
Fax 01625 610238

Useful Addresses

Those listed here are charities. Please enclose a stamped, addressed envelope when writing to them. Apart from those I have listed, there are numerous other such groups. A telephone business directory may list these, or you can find out more at your local library or Citizens' Advice Bureau.

AUSTRALIA

Association of Relatives and Friends of the Mentally Ill
311 Hay Street
Subiaco
Western Australia 6008

Help Call Service
1A Hamilton Street
Mount Albert
Victoria 3127

Life Line Centre
210 Pit Street
Sydney
New South Wales 2000

LifeLine
16 Hamilton Place
Bowen Hills
Queensland 4006

Marriage and Family Counselling Service
262 Pitt Street
Sydney
New South Wales 2000

Queensland Marriage Guidance Council
159 St Paul's Terrace
Brisbane
Queensland 4000

Samaritans
60 Bagot Road
Subiaco
Western Australia 6008

CANADA

Canadian Association for Marriage and Family Therapy
271 Russell Hill Road
Toronto
Ontario M4V 2T5

Canadian Mental Health Association
National Office, 3rd Floor
2160 Yonge Street
Toronto
Ontario M4S 2Z3

or

65 Brunswick Street
Fredericton
New Brunswick E3B 1G5

Suicide Distress Centre
Toronto Office
PO Box 395
Postal Station K
Toronto
Ontario M4P 2G7

NEW ZEALAND

Mental Health Foundation of New Zealand Inc
PO Box 37/438
Parnell
Auckland 1

SOUTH AFRICA

South African Federation for Mental Health
210 Happiness House
PO Box 2587
Loveday and Wolmarans Street
Johannesburg 200

or

PO Box 7
Observatory
Cape Town 7935

or

4th Floor, Maritime House
Salmon Grove
Durban 4001

UK

The Association for Post-Natal Illness
25 Jerdan Place
Fulham
London SW6 1BE
For information about forms of depression triggered by child-
 birth.

The Carers National Association
20/25 Glasshouse Yard
London, EC1A 4JS
Carersline 0171-490 8898
Provides support for carers.

CRUSE Bereavement Care
Cruse House
126 Sheen Road
Richmond
Surrey TW9 1UR
Bereavement Line 0181-332 7227
Provides support for those who are bereaved.

Depression Alliance
PO Box 1022
London SE1 7QB
Provides information, support and understanding for victims
and their carers.

The Defeat Depression Action Campaign
The Royal College of Psychiatrists
17 Belgrave Square
London SW1X 8PG
Set up to increase public awareness of depression and the fact
that it is treatable.

Depressives Anonymous
36 Chestnut Avenue
Beverley
Humberside HU17 9QU

Depressives Associated
PO Box 5
Castle Town
Portland
Dorset DT5 1BQ

The Manic Depressive Fellowship
13 Rosslyn Road
Twickenham TW1 2AR
Provides information for those involved with this particular
form of depression.

Mind
22 Harley Street
London W1N 2ED
Offers information about mental illness. They run a Saneline

giving information and support for carers and sufferers on
0171-724 8000

Relate
Herbert Gray College
Little Church Street
Rugby
Warks CV21 3AP
Deals with marital problems. There are local branches of Relate
in the telephone book.

SAD Association
PO Box 989
London SW7 2PZ
They provide information about Seasonal Affective Disorder. It
is possible to hire therapeutic lights from them.

The Samaritans
Offer help by telephone 24 hours a day for anyone who needs
to talk. Look for their local number in your telephone
book.

USA

Chronic Fatigue Syndrome Society
PO Box 230108
Portland
Oregon 97223

Compassionate Friends
PO Box 1347
Oak Brook
IL 60521
Help people to deal with the death of a child.

Emotional Health Anonymous
2420 San Gabriel Boulevard
Rosemead
CA 91770

Emotions Anonymous
PO Box 4245
St Paul
MN 55104

Foundation for Depression and Manic Depression
Seven E 67th Street
New York
NY 10021

Mothers are People Too
c/o ASPO/Lamaze
1411 K Street NW
Suite 200
Washington DC 20005
For depression associated with childbirth.

Samaritans
802 Boylston Street
Boston
MA 02199

Suicide Prevention Center of Los Angeles
1041 S Menlo Avenue
Los Angeles
CA 90006

Index

ELEMENT BOOKS LTD
PUBLISHERS

Element is an independent general publishing house. Our list includes titles on Religion, Personal Development, Health, Native Traditions, Modern Thought and Current Affairs, and is probably the most comprehensive collection of books in its sphere.

To order direct from Element Books, or to join the Element Club without obligation and receive regular details of great offers, please contact:
Customer Services, Element Books Ltd, Longmead, Shaftesbury, Dorset SP7 8PL, England.   Tel: 01747 851339   Fax: 01747 851394

Or you can order direct from your nearest distributor:

UK and Ireland
Penguin Group Distribution Ltd, Bath Road, Harmondsworth, Middlesex UB7 0DA, England.
Tel: 0181 899 4000
Fax: 0181 899 4020/4030

Canada
Penguin Books Canada Ltd, 10 Alcorn Avenue, Suite 300, Toronto, Ontario MV4 3B2.
Tel: (416) 925 2249
Fax: (416) 925 0068

Central & South America & the Caribbean
Humphrey Roberts Associates, 24 High Street, London E11 2AQ, England.
Tel: 0181 530 5028
Fax: 0181 530 7870

USA
Viking Penguin Inc, 375 Hudson Street, New York, NY 10014.
Tel: (212) 366 2000
Fax: (212) 366 2940

Australia
Jacaranda Wiley Ltd, PO Box 1226, Milton, Queensland 4064.
Tel: (7) 369 9755 Fax: (7) 369 9155

New Zealand
Forrester Books NZ Ltd, 3/3 Marken Place, Glenfield, Auckland 10.
Tel: 444 1948   Fax: 444 8199

Other areas:
Penguin Paperback Export Sales, 27 Wrights Lane, London W8 5TZ, England.
Tel: 0171 416 3000
Fax: 0171 416 3060

The Health Essentials Series

Comprehensive, high-quality introductions
to complementary healthcare

Each book in the *Health Essentials* series is written by a practising expert in their field, and presents all the essential information on each therapy, explaining what it is and how it works. Advice is also given, where possible, on how to begin using the therapy at home, together with comprehensive lists of courses and classes available worldwide.

In this series:

128/144 pages • 216 x 138 mm • Paperback • Line illustrations
UK £5.99 • USA $9.95 • Canada $12.99

The Natural Way Series

**Comprehensive guides to gentle, safe and effective treatments
for today's common illnesses**

Element's innovative *Natural Way* series provides practical and
authoritative information on holistic and orthodox treatments for our
most common illnesses. Endorsed by both the British Holistic
Medical Association and the American Holistic Medical Association,
these concise guides explain clearly what the disease is, how and why
it occurs, and what can be done about it. Each book includes advice
on helping yourself and where to turn to for outside qualified help.

In this series:

128/144 pages • 178 x 111 mm • Paperback • Line illustrations
UK £3.99 • USA $5.95 • Canada $7.99